Summer

ON

FAT PIG
FARM

MATTHEW
EVANS

Summer

ON

FAT PIG
FARM

MATTHEW
EVANS

MURDOCH BOOKS

CONTENTS

WELCOME

Summer comes slowly to our valley.
Sometimes we get a hint in mid spring, a day when the thermometer soars. Sometimes summer creeps in, frustratingly snail-like in pace, waiting to really warm up.

We time summer by various things: the flourishing of the elderflower, marking roughly the end of spring; the cutting of silage, a forerunner to hay; the starchiness of the broad beans after months of them being our major green; the fact we need to start watering the fruit trees after two seasons of letting nature do it for us.

Fat Pig Farm is one of the last farms in the local area to brown off as hot weather comes. Our little gully captures the wind, but the valley location means we retain a bit more moisture. Typically, it hardly rains in summer. We keep an eye on the water tanks. We watch the weather over the Huon River; the way the rain falls on Geeveston. In winter, rain comes belting across in minutes and sprays the windows, encouraging us to button up our jackets. In summer, the rain clouds seem to pause, to look over at our little farm, and then dissipate or go on down the Huon and leave us well alone.

Summer is most apparent on the plate. This is fruit season: we gorge on the stuff. From the first mulberries, through gooseberries to raspberries. We celebrate the first cherries of the year with pip-spitting competitions on the deck, my son and I shirtless so we don't stain our clothes. We buy trays of peaches and nectarines from the Cane family on the other side of the river; impossibly sweet, melting-flesh stone fruit—the sort that dribbles down your chin as you eat them, that peel at the mere touch of a hand. In a good year, we harvest masses of apricots and realise the commercial varieties really aren't the goods.

Summer means work. We milk all summer, and the cream is usually at its best then, which leads us into storing batches of butter for the leaner cold months. The garden needs watering most days. The pigs' wallows need filling, the cows' troughs are watched for faults in the siphon. Weeds grow well in our garden, protected from grazing by wallabies, so we spend quite a bit of time with the brush cutters and the Dutch hoe. And all the work is fuelled by our harvest. Blackberries late in the season, plucked from numerous fencelines. Raspberries, usually in two flushes: one at the start, the other on the cusp of autumn. Peas, so sugar-sweet straight from the pod. There's even the first of the new season's apples to be had, the sweet/sour gravenstein that gets baked into pies or simply devoured on the hoof.

But summer also means longer days. It means more chance to drop in a line or put up a tent. It means barbecues and cevaps, the scent of coals and fresh herbs, of fire-licked meats and charred veg.

Every year we can't believe the change. The need to water, the lack of mud. The (slightly sad) realisation that we don't actually have to light the cooker. The need for sunscreen. In midwinter, summer seems impossible. Then it lands with a thwack, with strawberries and blackcurrants, with stone fruit and corn.

Summer cooking often isn't cooking. It's assembling. Or gathering. Or gobbling in the garden. Summer cooking is drinking cider and sipping pinot gris. Cooking in the hot months is usually shorter and simpler, lighter and brighter. It's the gentlest season in the kitchen. All poaching and barely blanching, and dressing salads.

But most of all, every summer is a celebration of the bounty of the land.

CHAPTER 1

BRUNCH

In the warmer months, we think of second breakfasts after early morning chores (I think it's called 'brunch' for those of you not on the land). We're talking bacon butties and Afghan eggs; real crumpets; crisp waffles; drunken raspberries and no-machine ice cream. (Oh, right, that's dessert: it's a fine line…)

On warmer days it's enough to have a little trifle to make brunch an occasion. We're unlikely to have porridge, though we do sneak in a little sweetened polenta, which seems to have become ingrained in the routine all year around.

If we're having people over, it could be a Welsh rarebit—a nod to my heritage and the beauty of simple cheese on toast—a fresh farmhouse curd or even some still-warm ricotta made from Elsie's golden guernsey milk.

And if brunch becomes lunch, and a way to hide from the worst of the midday sun, so be it. The smoked trout kedgeree is just as lovely later in the day. That might even give me a chance to bake fresh honey buns to make a little bacon sandwich, too.

THE PERFECT SUMMER
BREAKFAST TRIFLE

SERVES 4

This dish, which is best made just before eating, was inspired by one I had at
The Old Cable Station at Stanley in Tassie's north west. The fruit you use can,
of course, evolve as the season progresses. Use blueberries and nectarines
if you have them, and raw muesli if the only toasted version is one of those
nasty, cheap, overly sweet ones.

150 g (5½ oz/1¼ cups) raspberries
1 tablespoon sugar
250 g (9 oz/1⅔ cups) strawberries, stems removed, halved
125 g (4½ oz/1 cup) toasted muesli
2 yellow peaches, stones removed, cut into bite-size pieces
100 g (3½ oz) natural yoghurt
   (try goat, sheep or buffalo if you can get it)
2 tablespoons honey
100 ml (3½ fl oz) pure cream (35% fat), lightly whipped

Pop the raspberries and sugar into a small saucepan and put it over a modest heat
to melt the fruit slightly. Remove from the heat and add the halved strawberries,
stirring well to coat. Set aside to cool.

Take four large tumblers and put a tablespoon of muesli in each one. Plop a
quarter of the peach pieces into each one then spoon the berries over evenly. Add
another tablespoon of muesli to each glass. Whisk the yoghurt with half the honey,
then stir in the cream. Spoon this mixture over the fruit and muesli, then top with
a little more muesli. Drizzle a tiny bit more honey over each glass and serve at room
temperature rather than heavily chilled.

BACON NUDGERS

PER PERSON

The Brits have so many wonderful names for different kinds of bread rolls—and the 'nudger' is one of my favourites. It's a light, elongated roll, and at Fat Pig Farm, we think the name suits our rolls filled with particularly smoky bacon and a bit of fresh mayonnaise. Sometimes we serve them at festivals or events. Mostly that's because we want to eat them ourselves.

1–2 rashers (slices) of bacon
1 light bread roll, ideally ciabatta style (or use Honey Buns, page 208)
1 tablespoon fresh mayonnaise (see page 20 and simply omit
the horseradish)

Remove the rind from the bacon and cut the rasher(s) in halves or thirds, depending on the size of the bacon and the roll.

Heat a frying pan over a medium heat. Fry the bacon gently until it starts to colour and the fat has surrendered to the pan.

Cut the bread roll in half, smear it well with mayonnaise and add the hot bacon. Eat it greedily while you make yourself another. Or a cup of tea.

WELSH RAREBIT

SERVES 4

Welsh rarebit is really just cheese on toast, but what cheese on toast! The beer and mustard turn this into a classy way to use up yesterday's bread. Original recipes use powdered mustard; I like the elegance of dijon, though a bit of hot English might liven it up too. Old recipes also use proper cheddar, but if you've a cheap, rubbery cheddar in the fridge and some good Italian parmesan, replace 50 g (1¾ oz) of the cheddar with 50 g (1¾ oz) of parmesan. When you serve this with a poached egg on top, it's called Welsh buck.

2 tablespoons beer
2–3 teaspoons dijon mustard
15 g (½ oz) butter
200 g (7 oz) good cheddar cheese, grated
pinch of cayenne pepper
1 teaspoon Worcestershire sauce
4 slices bread

Heat all the ingredients except the bread in a saucepan over gentle heat, and stir until the cheese has melted and the whole lot is one thick paste. It may not look smooth, and that's fine. It's going to taste wonderful, don't you worry. Sometimes it's easier to let this paste cool a tad before making the toast, although it can look slightly curdled as it cools, too.

Heat a griller (broiler) to maximum, and using a tray that only just holds the bread (it's great to catch the spillage later), toast the bread on one side. Turn the bread over, spread the other side with the cheese paste and grill until brown, ideally not too close to the grill element. I actually use the fan-forced griller in my oven, which works really well, with the bread on the second shelf down. Try to scrape off any spillage that ends up on the tray and hopefully isn't burnt, and serve the rarebit immediately, with the rest of the bottle of beer if so inclined.

BACON BUTTIES WITH HOMEMADE HORSERADISH MAYO, WATERCRESS & TOMATO

SERVES 4

Home-made bacon butties, using good smoky bacon, laced with horseradish and watercress, just taste better. You can add more horseradish once the mayonnaise is made if you need more of a kick. This recipe makes a generous amount of mayo, enough for plenty of bacon butties, but it's hard to make less as it's difficult to whisk a single egg yolk.

4 generous rashers (slices) of bacon
4 Honey Buns (see page 208), halved
cultured butter, for spreading
a few slices of fresh tomato
a handful of watercress

Horseradish mayo
2 egg yolks
2 teaspoons French-style mustard
2 teaspoons lemon juice
1 teaspoon finely grated lemon zest
1–2 teaspoons finely grated horseradish
250 ml (9 fl oz/1 cup) sunflower oil

To make the horseradish mayo, whisk the egg yolks with the mustard, lemon juice, lemon zest and horseradish in a large bowl that is fixed somehow: I find placing it over a saucepan with a tea towel (dish towel) in between tends to stop it moving much. The reason for this is that you need two hands for the mayo, and won't have a spare to hold the bowl. Put the oil into a jug with a narrow spout and pour a fine thread into the egg mix as you whisk. Continue whisking as you pour in the oil so the mixture becomes emulsified (doesn't split). If you start gently you can generally get faster with the oil towards the end.

Whisk until all the oil is incorporated, add ¼–⅓ teaspoon salt to taste and a splash of cold water at the end. Taste. The mayonnaise should be rich and a bit salty, but not overly so. If it's too rich, you can add more lemon juice or a splash of vinegar to cut the fattiness. Keeps well in a sterile container in the fridge for up to a week.

Fry the bacon well to your liking. Butter the buns nicely (or make toast), place the bacon on the bun bottoms and add sliced tomato and watercress. Spread the bun tops generously with horseradish mayo. Sandwich top and bottom together and eat while hot.

REAL CRUMPETS WITH LEATHERWOOD HONEY BUTTER
MAKES ABOUT A DOZEN

Home-made crumpets don't have as many holes as store-bought, and take a while to cook, but the good news is you can make them ahead of time because they are even better toasted a couple of days after making. You will need crumpet rings, which are available from good cookware stores.

750 ml (26 fl oz/3 cups) milk
7 g (¼ oz) sachet dried yeast
1 teaspoon caster (superfine) sugar
30 g (1 oz) butter, plus extra for cooking
500 g (1 lb 2 oz/3⅔ cups) plain (all-purpose) flour
1 teaspoon salt

Whipped honey butter
100 g (3½ oz) butter, softened
100 g (3½ oz) leatherwood or other floral honey

Warm the milk gently so that it feels the same temperature as your finger. Too hot and you'll kill the yeast. Dissolve the yeast in 2 tablespoons of the milk. Dissolve the sugar in the remaining milk. Melt the butter. Mix the flour and salt and stir in the milk and butter then the yeast. Stir until it's an even, fairly thick batter. Cover and leave in a warmish place to rise for 60–90 minutes. It should be bubbly and able to be poured, though slowly. Transfer to a large jug.

Grease the crumpet rings and a griddle or a large heavy-based frying pan. (Remember, butter tastes much better.) Heat gently over low to medium heat and pour the mixture about two-thirds of the way up the sides of the crumpet rings. The mixture will continue to rise so don't overfill the rings. Cook for 6–7 minutes on one side, so the top gets a few holes and has started to dry out, but don't let the base get too dark. A lower heat helps, but too low and the bubbles don't form as well. Remove the crumpet rings, turn crumpets over, then cook for 2–3 minutes on the other side to brown. Serve immediately or toast them later for a real treat.

To make the whipped honey butter, whip the butter and honey together until very light and fluffy. You could use a food processor for this, but a standmixer works best: depending on your mixer, you may find it easier to make a larger rather than smaller amount. Serve at room temperature but store any extra butter in the fridge.

PROPER YEAST WAFFLES WITH SALTY BUTTERSCOTCH PEARS

MAKES ABOUT 6 WAFFLES, DEPENDING ON THE SIZE OF YOUR WAFFLE IRON

The perfect waffle is one that is crisp on the outside and soft in the middle (not unlike some farmers I know). Keeping them warm in the oven, uncovered, while you cook the rest of the batter, actually helps gives the best result. But the secret is in the batter and the cooking. I like to use yeast in mine, and leave the batter to slowly come to life in the fridge overnight for a deeper flavour.

2 eggs, lightly beaten
375 ml (13 fl oz/1½ cups) milk
270 g (9½ oz/1¾ cups) plain (all-purpose) flour
1 teaspoon salt
1 teaspoon sugar
7 g (¼ oz) sachet dried yeast
Salty Butterscotch Pears (see page 30), for serving
perhaps some cream and maple syrup, for serving

Mix the eggs and milk in a large mixing bowl and whisk in the flour, salt, sugar and yeast until it forms a smooth batter. This batter will rise, so it's important to leave it in a bowl or container that is quite a bit larger than the original mix. Cover and refrigerate overnight, or for a few hours. If you're in a hurry, you can make the batter an hour before starting to use it, and leave it at room temperature, but it's simply not as good.

Heat a lightly buttered waffle pan and ladle the batter in. You may need to test the amount by cooking a few. Cook the waffles until they're golden brown and keep them warm on a plate in the oven on a low temperature.

Serve with the salty butterscotch pears, or any fruit that's in season (which could be strawberries, or other berries, or some fresh or poached peaches), and maple syrup and cream, if desired.

ROASTED PLUMS WITH DRAINED YOGHURT, HAZELNUTS & HONEY

SERVES 6

I quite adore the simplicity of these flavours. You have the warmth of the hazelnuts, the fragrance of honey, the tartness of plums and the richness of the yoghurt. Plus the textures are magic together. To get the very best out of the yoghurt, I drain it overnight, but if you're in a hurry, you could use Greek-style natural yoghurt instead.

500 g (1 lb 2 oz) natural yoghurt
500 g (1 lb 2 oz) plums, particularly blood plums and the like,
    halved, stones removed
3–4 tablespoons brown sugar
100 g (3½ oz/⅔ cup) roasted hazelnuts, chopped roughly
4 tablespoons honey, warmed slightly if thick, for drizzling

Line a colander with a clean cloth such as muslin (cheesecloth), place on a plate to catch drips and tip in the yoghurt. Cover with a lid or plastic wrap (to avoid things falling in, or other flavours getting in) and place in the fridge for several hours or overnight. This will drain out a lot of whey and leave a richer, thicker result.

Preheat the oven to 220°C (425°F). Wash the plums. Lay out evenly in one layer on a baking tray and sprinkle with the sugar. Bake in the centre of the oven for about 15 minutes until soft and starting to brown.

Put some plums in the bottom of six jars. Use half the yoghurt on top, then add the remaining plums, then the last of the yoghurt. Top with the nuts and drizzle the honey over. Serve at room temperature.

Summer sucks moisture from the ground,
from the leaves, from us as we lug pails
and dig ground and move cows.

AFGHAN EGGS WITH GARLICKY LENTILS & PITTA

SERVES 4

It may not look all that flash—a mangle of red sauce with the eggs bubbling away in it, atop some grey lentils—but the flavours are robust, wonderful and worth getting out of bed for. Or getting out of bed to make it, if you're the cook in the house.

1 tablespoon olive oil
1 small red (Spanish) onion, peeled and diced
1 small red capsicum (pepper), seeds removed, cut into strips
½ teaspoon cumin seeds
400 g (14 oz/about 2 large) tomatoes, diced
1 tablespoon dried mint
4 eggs
pitta bread, for serving

Garlicky lentils

1–2 tablespoons olive oil
2 garlic cloves, crushed
1 small celery stalk, finely diced
1 red chilli, finely chopped
215 g (7⅝ oz/1 cup) green lentils
500–750 ml (17–26 fl oz/2–3 cups) water
1 cinnamon stick

To make the garlicky lentils, heat the oil in a medium saucepan over low heat and fry the garlic for a minute with the celery and chilli. Add the lentils and water, pop in the cinnamon stick and cook for 30–40 minutes until the lentils are tender, adding more water if necessary. Season well with salt and pepper and keep warm.

To make the capsicum mixture, heat the oil in a medium frying pan over moderately high heat. Fry the onion well for a few minutes, stirring often, until it starts to colour. Add the capsicum and continue frying until it goes really soft, turning down the heat if necessary. Add the cumin seeds and fry for a minute, stirring regularly. Stir in the tomatoes and mint with some salt and pepper and cook for another 10 minutes, adding a splash of water if necessary. You want the sauce to be thick, but not quite as thick as porridge, by the end.

When ready to serve, transfer the lentils to a medium frying pan, spoon the capsicum mixture into the centre and bring it to a good simmer. Crack in the eggs and cook to your liking; I sometimes put a lid on to help them cook more evenly. Spoon portions of the mixture onto plates and serve with warmed pitta bread.

SWEET POLENTA WITH SALTY BUTTERSCOTCH PEARS

SERVES 2–3

Just a yummy concoction of warm polenta and sweet pears that makes getting out of bed far easier to contemplate. Pears only come in at the end of summer. Before that, we have this with lightly warmed strawberries!

500 ml (17 fl oz/2 cups) water
500 ml (17 fl oz/2 cups) milk
200 g (7 oz/1 cup) polenta
generous pinch of salt
good knob (a bit over 1 tablespoon) of butter
2 tablespoons sugar
1 tablespoon good-quality honey

Salty butterscotch pears
150 g (5½ oz/¾ cup lightly packed) dark brown sugar
1 cinnamon stick
80 g (2¾ oz) butter
100 ml (3½ fl oz) cream
big pinch of sea salt
3 pears, unpeeled, cut into quarters and cored

To make the salty butterscotch pears, heat the sugar and cinnamon stick in a large frying pan over low heat for 5–10 minutes, stirring often. You want the sugar to start to catch just a bit. Add the butter and beat it in until smooth, then add the cream and salt and whisk until smooth. Add the pears and cook in the caramel until tender.

To make the polenta, heat the water and milk in a generous saucepan over high heat. As it comes to a simmer, sprinkle in the polenta through your fingers, stirring the whole time. You don't want it to clump up. Stir until it comes back to the boil, then turn the heat right down and simmer for 10 minutes, stirring occasionally. The polenta should have a nice porridge-like consistency by this stage, so add more water if necessary. Add the salt, butter, sugar and honey and stir to mix in well. Serve hot with the salty butterscotch pears.

CURDS & WHEY WITH GINGER APRICOT SYRUP

SERVES 4

This recipe is for a fresh farmhouse curd cheese, something we make with our own milk, but you can easily do it with purchased milk. It's incredibly light and refreshing, not unlike that sensational soy curd they serve at the end of yum cha in Chinese restaurants. The ginger apricot syrup is delicious poured over vanilla ice cream or pancakes, or pop a few tablespoons in a glass and top with soda water for a refreshing apricot sparkler.

1 junket (rennet) tablet
1 tablespoon cold water
500 ml (17 fl oz/2 cups) milk

Ginger apricot syrup
500 g (1 lb 2 oz) apricots, halved, stone removed
500 ml (17 fl oz/2 cups) water
250 g (9 oz) sugar
3 cm (1¼ inch) knob of ginger, smashed

To make the apricot and ginger syrup, purée the apricots and water in a blender. Pour the purée into a large saucepan with the sugar and stir over medium heat until the sugar dissolves. Add the ginger and bring to the boil. Reduce the heat and simmer for 5 minutes, gently skimming any foam off the top.

Remove from the heat and allow to cool. Fish out the ginger with a spoon, and skim off and discard any remaining foam on the surface. Pour the syrup into a couple of jars and use it immediately or refrigerate for up to a week.

To make the curds and whey, crush the junket tablet and dissolve in the water. In a medium saucepan over low heat gently warm the milk to lukewarm (37°C/100°F): if the milk gets too hot, allow it to cool (a watched pot never boils, but an unwatched pot of milk will). If you don't have a thermometer, 37°C (100°F) is about the same temperature as your body, so if you touch the outside of the saucepan, it should feel the same temperature as your hand.

Remove the milk from the heat and stir through the dissolved junket tablet, stirring quickly for a few seconds only, then pour into a large serving bowl. Allow to stand in a warm place for about 15 minutes to let the junket set. It's important that you don't disturb the junket at all while it sets. When it's firm, place it in the fridge to chill.

To serve, run a knife through the junket to break up the curds. Spoon the curds and whey into a serving bowl and drizzle with cooled apricot syrup.

SMOKED TROUT KEDGEREE

SERVES 4–6

This is a variation on the British egg dish often made with smoked fish. Here we've used smoked trout, although I've also done it with smoked eel, which is pretty amazing, too. It makes things easier if you wrap the cardamom and cloves in a little muslin (cheesecloth) so you can easily remove them after cooking without having to search through the rice.

6 eggs
1 small and 1 large onion
olive oil or sunflower oil, for frying
200 g (7 oz/1 cup) basmati rice
2 whole cardamom pods
2 whole cloves
8–10 fresh curry leaves,
    if available
pinch of salt
375 ml (13 fl oz/1½ cups) water
2 teaspoons red or brown
    mustard seeds

1 teaspoon garam masala
½ teaspoon cumin seeds
¼ teaspoon turmeric
30 g (1 oz) butter
200 g (7 oz) smoked trout fillet,
    broken into large bite-size
    pieces and carefully picked
    over for bones
1 tablespoon chopped flat-leaf
    (Italian) parsley, for serving

Boil the eggs for 6 minutes, drain, cool in cold water, then peel and break up roughly with a fork. Set to one side.

Slice the small onion thinly and fry over a moderately high heat in about 2 tablespoons of the oil until dark brown but not acrid, drain well on paper towel and set aside to cool and crisp up a bit.

Rinse and drain the rice. Put it in a small saucepan with the cardamom, cloves, curry leaves, salt and water. Cover with a tight fitting lid, bring to the boil, then reduce the heat to low, and cook for 12 minutes. Turn off the heat and, after about 5–10 minutes, open the lid, scoop out the cardamom and cloves, and use a fork to gently fluff the rice.

Slice and fry the large onion in olive oil for about 5 minutes until it is starting to colour. Stir in the remaining spices and fry them for a minute, stirring pretty much constantly. Don't let the spices burn. Add the butter, eggs and rice to the pan with the spiced onions and mix with a fork. Fold in the trout and serve warm or at room temperature topped with the parsley and the crisp fried onions, seasoned with freshly milled black pepper to taste.

HONEYED RICOTTA WITH ROASTED NUTS

SERVES 2

This is a sensational light brunch: clouds of still vaguely warm ricotta drizzled with honey and given the snap of roasted nuts are a pure delight. This dish doesn't fuel us through a day of farm chores, but it does make us very happy on a slower summer morning. Unlike good deli ricotta, which is made from whey, this version uses whole milk and a touch of cream. It's far superior to the long-life stuff they sell as ricotta in supermarkets. If you don't make your own ricotta, buy 250 g (9 oz) good-quality real ricotta from a deli and warm it gently just before eating.

2 tablespoons runny honey
3–4 tablespoons roasted nuts (almonds, pistachios
    and hazelnuts or walnuts), roughly chopped

Home-made whole milk ricotta
2 litres (70 fl oz/8 cups) milk
100 ml (3½ fl oz) cream
2 tablespoons white vinegar
125 ml (4 fl oz/½ cup) water

To make the milk ricotta, place the milk and cream in a 3 litre (105 fl oz/12 cup) saucepan over decent heat, stirring gently a couple of times to avoid it catching, until it's about 93°C (200°F). The best way to check this without a thermometer is to bring it to the point where it has foam on top, but isn't quite boiling.

Mix the vinegar with the water, turn up the heat on the milk to full, then quickly stir the vinegar mixture into the hot milk and whisk just for a second or two. Stop whisking straightaway and remove the pan from the heat. The milk should curdle immediately, and form a raft of clotted curds on top. This will be your ricotta. Let it clump up (this makes it much easier to remove) then lift it off gently with a slotted spoon, or similar. Drain through muslin (cheesecloth) or sturdy paper towel lining a sieve.

Tip the drained ricotta onto a plate, or spoon into bowls. Dribble over the honey, and top with the roasted nuts. Serve at room temperature for brekky, for brunch or even as a dessert.

BREAKFAST TARTS WITH BROWN SUGAR & APPLE BUTTER

MAKES 12

Apple butter is long-cooked apple that goes dark from serious slow cooking. It's luscious as is, and a great use for out-of-season apples that have gone a bit soft. Or you could use some of the salty butterscotch pears (page 30) for these tarts.

300 g (10½ oz) sweet shortcrust pastry (see page 224)
12 tablespoons Apple Butter (see below)
2 tablespoons brown sugar
1 tablespoon butter
1 apple, thinly sliced

Preheat the oven to 200°C (400°F). Roll the shortcrust pastry out to fit a dozen holes in a shallow cupcake tin, or similar. Add a little apple butter to each one. Melt the brown sugar and butter in a small saucepan. While it melts, lay a couple of slices of apple over the apple butter in each tartlet. Spoon a little of the brown sugar butter over each one and bake in the centre of the oven for 10–15 minutes until brown. Serve as soon as they cool. The apple butter tends to send the pastry soft: if you want to save the tarts, use a sturdier pastry rather than a very short one.

▼ ▼

APPLE BUTTER

There's no point making a small amount of apple butter, so here's enough to use in a few things or a lot of tarts.

2 kg (4 lb 8 oz) apples, peeled, cored and roughly diced
about 100–200 g (3½–7 oz) sugar, depending on apple variety

Preheat the oven to 180°C (350°F).

Put the apples in a large ovenproof dish or pan with a tiny splash of water and allow the apples to cook right down, stirring often. You want most of the liquid to evaporate out, and the apple to darken as it caramelises slightly, but not burn. We sometimes put it into the oven for a few hours to do a long, gentle cook, but you could, in theory, do it on the stove top. When it's nearly done, add the sugar and then be careful as this may catch and burn more easily now. Store this apple butter in sterile jars in the fridge for up to a month. Use on crumpets, smeared on fruit toast, in tarts or as part of a dessert or pudding.

CHAPTER

2

LIGHT THINGS

We don't really do stodgy food in summer.
Just food without too many fussy components, or a fresh one-dish meal. Everything from a snack of watermelon with chilli and lime, to a pork taco. I tend to use a bit more spice in the warmer months, perhaps to lace black beans or meatballs. Capsicum and corn and avocado are on the menu, even though we tend to buy the capsicums and avocados in. Tomatoes, of course, make their presence felt (although our real glut is in autumn), moistening flash-fried prawns or just chopped and put on oily, garlicky, properly chargrilled bruschetta.

Meals tend to be more mobile, be it a roasted chicken wrapped in a cider-soaked towel, torn apart while sitting on the back of the ute; or a pie, perhaps in home-made filo pastry, that can be just as nice after it's cooled as when it's served hot.

Most of all, the meals don't weigh us down. Whether it's croque madame—with its cheesy, eggy bread—or a little mushroom pie, the idea is to have flavoursome food that doesn't sit like a dead weight when you head off to fish or shift a cow's trough or set up the tent near the dam. It's food where there's always just enough room for a little bit more, in case someone's made dessert.

MUSHROOM HAND PIES

MAKES 16 SMALL PIES

We preserve the mushrooms we collect in summer: sliced and dried they add a wonderful flavour to stews and braises all year. In their place, use mixed fresh mushrooms and a small amount of dried porcini mushrooms.

125 ml (4 fl oz/½ cup) boiling water
10 g (⅜ oz) dried porcini mushrooms, sliced
knob of butter
1 small red (Spanish) onion, finely diced
2 garlic cloves, crushed
1 thyme sprig
100 g (3½ oz/2 cups) mixed mushrooms, such as button, shiitake and oyster, chopped
2 tablespoons white wine (optional)

50 g (1¾ oz) parmesan cheese, grated
1 egg, lightly beaten with a little salt and a drop of water

Butter pastry
250 g (9 oz/1⅔ cups) plain (all-purpose) flour
220 g (7¾ oz) butter, chilled
1 egg
1–2 tablespoons iced water

To make the butter pastry, rub the flour and butter together well until the mixture looks like breadcrumbs. You could do it in a food processor, ideally with a chilled blade. Add the egg and just enough iced water to make a dough. Knead just until it comes together and refrigerate for 30 minutes before using.

Preheat the oven to 190°C (375°F). In a small bowl, pour the boiling water over the porcini mushrooms and stand for 15 minutes. Drain, reserving the soaking water.

Melt the butter in a large frying pan over medium heat and fry the onion until soft. Add the garlic and thyme and cook for few more minutes. Add the chopped fresh mushrooms and cook for 5 minutes or until tender. Add the porcini mushrooms with their soaking water and cook for 5 minutes or until the water has evaporated. (You could add the white wine here, then cook until the wine has evaporated.)

Remove from the heat, season a little cautiously with salt and pepper (the cheese adds some salt), then stir the parmesan cheese through and set aside to cool.

On a lightly floured surface, roll out the pastry to about 5 mm (¼ inch) thick. Use an 8 cm (3¼ inch) pastry cutter to cut out 16 circles. Place a heap of mushroom mix in the centre of eight of the circles. Brush the edges with the beaten egg, then top with the remaining circles of pastry. Seal the edges by crimping with a fork or pressing with your fingers. Cut a small vent in the top of each pie with a pair of kitchen scissors.

Brush the tops with the beaten egg and bake in the oven for 20 minutes or until golden brown.

VITELLO TONNATO
SERVES 8

Vitello tonnato is, classically, poached veal topped with a tuna sauce. It's light and bright, and in Italy they often cook the veal for well over an hour. I prefer it still pink. You can roast the veal if you don't want to poach it and some people like to use chicken or pork instead of veal. The inserting of the anchovies into the veal is a bit of an extra step, but I like the flavour they impart. Omit it if you're in a hurry.

9 anchovies
1 kg (2 lb 4 oz) rose veal loin
185 g (6½ oz) tinned tuna, in oil
2 egg yolks
250 ml (9 fl oz/1 cup) sunflower oil, or similar light-flavoured oil
1½ tablespoons lemon juice
30 g (1 oz) salted capers, soaked in warm water for 30 minutes, then well drained
a little parsley, roughly chopped (optional)

Cut 6 of the anchovies in half and push them into narrow slits you make in the veal with a knife.

Place the veal in a saucepan with enough boiling salted water to cover and barely simmer for 10 minutes (you can flavour the water with celery, parsley, carrot and peppercorns, or use stock). Cool in the water.

Drain the tuna and keep the oil. In a food processor, blend the tuna, the remaining 3 anchovies and the egg yolks until smooth. With the motor running, add the sunflower oil in a thin stream until well incorporated. Add the tuna oil and the lemon juice, also with the motor running. Taste and season with salt and pepper if needed.

To serve, thinly slice the veal. Smear half the tuna sauce onto a serving platter, lay the sliced veal on top, spread the remaining sauce over it and scatter with capers, and parsley, if using.

CIDER-SOAKED CHICKEN

SERVES 4

This is an old way of making a roast chicken taste more lively, simply by wrapping the just-roasted bird in a cider-soaked cloth and taking it on a picnic. On the drive to the picnic spot the cider perfumes the chicken meat. In France, they might use verjuice; cider in parts of the UK; and you could use a decent beer, too. Because I live in an apple-growing region, I've gone for a little cider myself.

> 1.8 kg (4 lb/no. 18) free-range chicken
> olive oil, for brushing
> about 150 ml (5 fl oz) dry cider
> Meyer Mayonnaise (see page 55), for serving

Lightly oil the chicken and season well with salt and pepper. Roast the chicken as you normally would in a 180°C (350°F) oven for about an hour. When it's cooked, soak a clean tea towel (dish towel) in water, wring it out, then soak it in enough cider so that it's a bit wet and dripping madly. Wrap the chicken in this cloth so it steams in the cider a bit. Take the chicken on a picnic, in a clean tray, and eat at room temperature or while still warm, with meyer mayonnaise as a dipping sauce or to moisten bread to eat it with.

IRANIAN-STYLE VERMICELLI RICE

SERVES 4

A classic Middle Eastern dish, this is a textural marvel, and it's really quite yummy with or without an accompaniment (though a little yoghurt dressing goes nicely). Try it with the cevaps (page 104), or some lightly barbecued lamb chops, perhaps with the zucchini mint salad (page 97).

40 g (1½ oz) butter

1 large onion, finely diced

2 cinnamon sticks

8 green cardamom pods

100 g (3½ oz) vermicelli (even better if you can get the sort from specialist Middle Eastern stores)

380 g (13½ oz/scant 2 cups) basmati rice

625 ml (21½ fl oz/2½ cups) water

Heat the butter in a large saucepan and gently fry the onion well with the spices. Break up the vermicelli into shortish lengths, add to the onion and fry until it starts to colour. Add the rice, fry for a minute or so longer, then tip in the water and season with salt and black pepper. Cover, bring to the boil, then turn the heat right down and simmer for 10 minutes. Turn off, but leave it on the stove (and DON'T remove the lid) for another 5–10 minutes. Fluff with a fork and serve warm.

MY CROQUE MADAME
MAKES 2

A good toasted cheese sandwich is a good toasted cheese sandwich. If you give it a French name, can we call it dinner? A croque madame is a croque monsieur with the addition of an egg.

4 thick slices of quality white bread
2 teaspoons dijon mustard
2 tablespoons sour cream, full-fat if you want the best effect
pinch of paprika, perhaps the hot version
2 slices gruyère cheese
6–8 rocket (arugula) leaves, washed
2 thin slices leg ham
lashings of butter, for spreading
2 eggs, fried or poached to your liking

Lay the bread on the work surface. Mix the mustard, sour cream, paprika and a goodly amount of freshly milled black pepper. Top two slices of bread with the cheese, then spread with the sour cream mix. Lay rocket on top, cover with ham and place the remaining bread slices on top of the lot.

Butter the top of each sandwich, then turn them over as you slide them into a coolish frying pan over medium heat and gently fry until brown. Butter the other piece of bread before turning over and browning the other side. I sometimes cover the pan to help the sandwiches cook more evenly. Place each sandwich on a plate, top with an egg and serve warm, and often.

RISI E BISI
SERVES 4 AS A STARTER

While those in Venice do love their risotto all'onda (wavy, meaning runny) risi e bisi isn't actually risotto. It's Venetian dialect for 'rice and peas', and is a cross between a runny risotto and a soup. The good thing for those with ankle biters or other pressing matters like making a white peach drink (page 232) is that, unlike risotto, it doesn't need constant stirring.

> 2 tablespoons butter
> 1 onion, finely chopped
> 2 tablespoons coarsely chopped flat-leaf (Italian) parsley
> 4 slices prosciutto, cut into bits
> 200 g (7 oz) risotto rice
> 1½ litres (52 fl oz/6 cups) chicken stock
>   (use water rather than purchased stock)
> 250 g (9 oz/1⅔ cups) peas (frozen is fine)
> 50 g (1¾ oz) parmesan cheese, grated

Heat the butter in a large saucepan and fry the onion gently until soft. Stir in the parsley and prosciutto and continue frying, without colouring the onion, for about 5 minutes more.

Add the rice and cook for 2 minutes then stir in the stock and some pepper. Simmer, stirring occasionally, for 10 minutes, then add the peas. Continue cooking for another 10 minutes or so until the rice is cooked through. If you need more liquid, add water or chicken stock. Stir in the cheese and serve hot.

WARM POTATO SALAD WITH PAPRIKA, ROASTED CAPSICUM & GOAT'S CURD

SERVES 4–6

This is a gentle summer salad to go with ham (post-Christmas), poached chicken (page 84), barbecued fish (such as the leatherjacket on page 95), other meats and the like.

1 large red capsicum (pepper)
1 large green capsicum (pepper)
2 tablespoons extra virgin olive oil
500 g (1 lb 2 oz) dutch cream or pink eye potatoes, scrubbed well
1 tablespoon sweet paprika
1 tablespoon apple cider vinegar
200 g (7 oz) goat's curd

Preheat the oven to 220°C (425°F).

Rub the capsicums with a tiny bit of the olive oil and roast in the middle of the oven, turning so they brown on all sides. Remove from the oven, pop into a bowl, cover with plastic and let them steam for a few minutes until cool enough to handle. Carefully remove the skin and seeds and discard them. Keep the cooking juices and cut the flesh into rough squares about bite size. Whatever you do, don't rinse the capsicums when you peel them or you'll wash off all the flavour.

Cut the potatoes into chunks if need be, or leave them whole if small. You want them evenly sized for cooking. Pop them into a saucepan with enough water to cover and a teaspoon of salt. Bring to the boil, turn down to a simmer and cook until tender. Drain, then toss the hot potatoes with the paprika, the capsicums and their cooking juices, the remaining olive oil and the vinegar. Taste and season with salt and pepper. At this point you can put it into a serving bowl and dot the curd on top, or even toss the curd through so it forms part of the dressing.

DILL & LEMON STEAMED CRABS WITH MEYER MAYO

SERVES 4–6

Fresh crabs—cooked in a dill-scented stock and served with rich lemony mayonnaise made from wonderful meyer lemons—make a simple, impressive feast. If you can't find uncooked crabs, use cooked: don't boil them, and add some dill to the mayonnaise. Then get ready to lick your fingers as you eat.

2 kg (4 lb 8 oz) whole uncooked
    crabs
80 g (2¾ oz/1 bunch) dill,
    coarsely chopped
1 lemon, sliced
1–2 lemons, extra, for squeezing

Meyer mayonnaise
juice and finely grated zest
    of ½ small meyer lemon
2 egg yolks
1 teaspoon mustard
125 ml (4 fl oz/½ cup)
    vegetable oil
125 ml (4 fl oz/½ cup)
    extra virgin olive oil
1 tablespoon hot water

To make the meyer mayonnaise, whisk the lemon juice, zest and egg yolks in a medium bowl with the mustard until smooth. Add the combined oils in a trickle and continue whisking while you add the oil in a stream, getting faster with the stream as you go. When all the oil is added, whisk in the hot water. Taste, add salt and freshly milled black pepper if needed, and allow to sit for a few hours in the fridge for better flavour. Store any leftover mayo in a sterile jar in the fridge, and use it up quickly. View it as a treat: a wonderful condiment to rejoice in for just a couple of days after making.

Put the crabs in a large stockpot that has a tight-fitting lid. Add water to a depth of about 2 cm (¾ inch) from the base of the stockpot. Sprinkle the dill and scatter the sliced lemon over the top. Put the pot over very high heat, bring to the boil and then put the lid on. Turn the heat down to medium and cook for about 5 minutes, until the crabs have changed colour completely, perhaps jiggling the pot a couple of times to ensure the crabs cook more evenly. Remove the lid when the crabs are cooked, and serve with the meyer mayonnaise and halved lemons for squeezing.

BUTTER-BRAISED PEAS & LEEKS WITH BRESAOLA & SAGE

SERVES 6 AS A SIDE DISH

Summer leeks are quite sweet, and this dish brings out their gentle flavour. Bresaola is a cut of cured beef. You can use good prosciutto in its place.

4 medium leeks, pale parts only, well washed
100 ml (3½ fl oz) water
2–3 tablespoons butter
2 teaspoons lemon juice
white pepper
about 20 sage leaves
155 g (5½ oz/1 cup) peas (fresh are good, frozen are fine)
4 slices bresaola
extra virgin olive oil, for serving (optional)
lemon wedges, for serving

Cut the leeks into 5 cm (2 inch) long chunks and lay them in a deep frying pan or flameproof casserole dish just big enough to fit them all in one layer. Add the water, butter, lemon juice and some salt and the white pepper to taste. Bring the juices to the boil over high heat. Throw in half the sage leaves, pop a lid on, turn down and barely simmer for about 10–15 minutes until the leeks are tender. (The cooking time can vary widely depending on how young and sweet the leeks are.) Throw in the remaining sage and the peas and bring to the boil without the lid on. Turn off the heat and allow the leeks to cool for just a few minutes in the pan juices until warm, or serve them hot.

Serve the leeks with slices of bresaola or strips cut from the slices. Perhaps drizzle the leeks with a little top-shelf extra virgin olive oil and be sure to offer some lemon wedges for squeezing.

Before you know it the grass has browned off, the creek has dried up and the sun lingers seemingly forever into the evenings, lending itself to lazy long dinners.

FISH IN ACQUA PAZZA
(CHUNKY TOMATO, BASIL & OIL SAUCE)
SERVES 8

Acqua pazza means crazy water, and is called that, supposedly, because of the way the oil and tomato form crazy patterns in the sauce. Thing is, you'd be crazy not to use this sauce in summer, when tomatoes are at their prime and you want a luscious light flavour in your dishes.

100 ml (3½ fl oz) extra virgin olive oil
2 garlic cloves, sliced
4 tomatoes, chopped
375 ml (13 fl oz/1½ cups) water
1 long red chilli, thinly sliced (optional)
1 kg (2 lb 4 oz/about 2 fillets) skinless fish fillets (such as morwong, barramundi or pink ling)
1 cup basil leaves, coarsely torn

Heat 1 tablespoon of the oil over low–medium heat and fry the garlic for 1 minute or until fragrant but not brown. Add the tomatoes and fry for a further minute. Pour in the water, add the chilli, if using, and cook for 5 minutes or until the tomatoes are just soft. Season with salt and pepper, and keep warm.

Heat 1 tablespoon of the oil in a large frying pan over medium–high heat. Cook the fish fillets for 3 minutes each side or until just cooked.

Stir the remaining oil into the warm tomato sauce, then pour the sauce over the fish. Scatter with the basil. (Alternatively, poach the fish in the sauce in a covered frying pan over low heat for 20 minutes or until just cooked.)

A LUSCIOUS TOMATO BRUSCHETTA

PER PERSON

The problem with most bruschetta is that the bread isn't very good, the bread is toasted rather than grilled and the topping is too tricked up or not made from top-notch ingredients. At the height of the tomato season, all you need is the taste of summer. The oil is essential. Don't buy cheap or 'light' oil: it'll be guaranteed to disappoint. If you don't end up licking oil and tomato off your fingers as you eat, the topping isn't indulgent enough.

> 1 large, properly ripe roma (plum) tomato
> 2 basil leaves, torn into small pieces
> 1 tablespoon extra virgin olive oil
> 2 fat, hand-cut slices of sourdough bread

Cut the tomato into a dice, about 7 mm (¼ inch) across. Sprinkle it with salt, add some freshly milled black pepper and the basil leaves, then toss well. Add the olive oil and mix well. Leave it to stand for half an hour. If you don't do this, you won't be getting the best result.

When ready to eat, you need to *abbrustolito* your bread. That is, you need to char it somewhat. A ridged pan, a barbecue hotplate, or even a flat cast-iron pan all work. Get your pan or barbecue hot, press the bread into it, and stop just before the bread goes black. Pale, insipid chargrilling won't give you that amazing flavour combo with the tomato and oil.

Spoon the tomato mixture generously over the bread and eat it warm or at room temperature.

A HUMMUS TO STOP YOU BUYING ONE FROM A SHOP

MAKES ABOUT 1 KG (2 LB 4 OZ)

This recipe makes a generous amount, which is perfectly fine because hummus tastes better if left to sit for a day or two. Tinned chickpeas don't do the recipe justice, so try to do it from scratch or even use a pressure cooker to speed things up. A good trick is to use 1 teaspoon of bicarbonate of soda (baking soda) in the cooking water to make the chickpeas soften more easily.

200 g (7 oz) dried chickpeas, soaked overnight if possible
1 litre (35 fl oz/4 cups) water
1 onion, halved
2 bay leaves
4–5 garlic cloves
1 tablespoon tahini (sesame seed paste)
3 tablespoons extra virgin olive oil, plus extra for serving
2–3 tablespoons lemon juice, to taste
1 teaspoon salt
¼ teaspoon ground cumin
paprika, for serving

If you haven't soaked the chickpeas, that's fine, they'll just take longer to cook. Either way, rinse the chickpeas and put them in a decent-size saucepan with the water, onion and bay leaves. Bring to the boil, then simmer, covered, for 1–2 hours or until very soft. Add more water, if necessary, to keep the chickpeas covered.

Drain, reserving the cooking liquid but discarding the bay leaves and onion.

Blend the garlic in a food processor and add some of the still-hot chickpeas. Hot chickpeas are important: they don't make such a fine paste if they've gone cold.

Purée the remaining ingredients and chickpeas, taking care not to overload the machine and adding some chickpea cooking liquid to produce a smooth, but not too runny, paste. You'll probably have to do it in batches to suit your machine.

Mix all the batches up together in a big bowl, adding pepper to taste, then allow to cool. Check the consistency (it thickens slightly as it cools) and add more cooking liquid if necessary; check the seasoning (cold food needs more salt than hot food to taste as lively). Serve with a sprinkling of paprika and a drizzle of extra virgin olive oil.

EGGPLANT PIZZAIOLA
SERVES 4

The term pizzaiola in Italy implies a tomato and basil sauce (a pizzaiolo is a male pizza maker…). I've used it here for exactly that: mine uses smoked cheese to add intrigue and mystery, although you can use ordinary mozzarella too. Carnivores can replace the eggplant (or add to it) with a piece of thinly sliced chicken or veal.

4 slices eggplant (aubergines), 1 cm (⅜ inch) thick
extra virgin olive oil, for brushing and frying
1 large onion, peeled and finely chopped
1 tablespoon chopped parsley
2 garlic cloves, crushed or sliced
400 g (14 oz) tomatoes, chopped (use tinned out of season)
about 10 basil leaves, torn
about 40 g (1½ oz) smoked mozzarella cheese, sliced

Brush the eggplant with olive oil and roast, chargrill or fry until tender. Meanwhile, heat 1 tablespoon of olive oil in a wide-base frying pan and gently cook the onion and parsley until soft. Add the garlic and cook for another minute. Slurp in the tomato and simmer for about 10 minutes until it has a sauce-like consistency. Add a touch of water if it starts to dry out. Taste and add salt and freshly milled black pepper if needed. When ready to eat, add the basil, then nestle the eggplant slices in the sauce. (It's possible to do this last step in the oven, too.) Top each eggplant slice with cheese, cover the pan with a lid and allow the cheese to melt a bit. Serve hot with bread or a simple rice pilaff.

FLASH-FRIED PRAWNS WITH TOMATO, BAY & GARLIC

SERVES 4 AS PART OF A TAPAS-STYLE MEAL

I just adore prawns, even though none of the ones in the shops come from my island home. I buy frozen raw prawns for this recipe and thaw them myself because, unless you're very close to the source, frozen actually does make a better uncooked product. (They degrade VERY quickly once caught.) If you don't want to make such a mess, you can prepare the sauce and just oven-roast the prawns in small pans in the sauce, or fry the prawns and then stir it all up together as I've suggested here.

3 tablespoons extra virgin olive oil
3 fresh bay leaves
5–6 garlic cloves, lightly crushed
210 g (7½ oz) tomatoes, peeled and diced (tinned is okay out of season)
300 g (10½ oz) peeled raw prawns (shrimp)
bread, for serving

Heat 2 tablespoons of the oil in a medium frying pan with the bay leaves over a moderately high heat until the leaves start to change colour slightly. Add the garlic and cook until it just starts to colour. Stir in the tomato and fry well to break it down to a roughish sauce, adding 3 tablespoons of water and a touch more as it cooks, if need be. What you want is an oily, garlicky, tomatoey sauce that will coat the prawns a bit.

In a clean frying pan, heat the remaining oil over a fierce heat and fry the prawns quickly on both sides. Pour in the sauce, tossing constantly, just long enough for the prawns to change colour and be well coated. Serve hot with torn bread.

BABY MEATBALLS WITH SMOKED PAPRIKA IN A SAFFRON CAPSICUM SAUCE

SERVES 5–6 AS A PART OF A TAPAS-STYLE MEAL

Lightly smoky pork meatballs are smothered in a summery capsicum sauce laced with saffron. Leftovers go really well on a bread roll for lunch, so perhaps make a double batch. You don't have to roast the capsicums first; you could fry them, but roasting gives a more intense, toasty character.

a generous pinch of saffron
80 ml (2½ fl oz/⅓ cup) dry white wine
500 g (1 lb 2 oz) minced (ground) pork
50 g (1¾ oz) pancetta or prosciutto, finely diced
2 eggs
50 g (1¾ oz/about ½ cup) fresh breadcrumbs
1 teaspoon sweet smoked paprika
pinch of ground nutmeg
3–4 tablespoons extra virgin olive oil
1 large red (Spanish) onion, peeled and finely sliced
5–6 garlic cloves, peeled and sliced
1 each red, green and yellow capsicums (peppers), seeded and roasted, then cut into narrow strips, 3 cm (1¼ inch) long
300 g (10½ oz) tomatoes, peeled and well chopped (use tinned if the season hasn't quite started yet)

Soak the saffron in the white wine overnight or as long as you can.

Meanwhile, mix the pork with the pancetta, eggs, breadcrumbs, paprika and nutmeg until well combined. Add 1 teaspoon of salt and mix well again. Cover and refrigerate well for at least half an hour. When chilled, use wet hands to roll the pork mince into little balls, about the diameter of a large coin (3 cm/1¼ inches). Chill again until ready to fry.

For the sauce, heat half the oil in a large heavy-based frying pan over moderate heat and fry the onion well for about 5 minutes until softening and just starting to brown. Add the garlic and cook for another minute or three. Stir in the capsicum and fry a little with ¼ teaspoon of salt until it starts to dry a bit. Stir in the tomato and fry to break it down a little. Add the saffron and its soaking wine and simmer, stirring occasionally, until the capsicum is breaking down and the tomato thickens the sauce a bit. Perhaps add a little water to help it all cook nicely. Taste for salt and pepper.

To serve, fry the meatballs to brown, preferably in a cast iron pan, and transfer them to the sauce with the remaining olive oil. Cover the pan with a lid and simmer, turning occasionally, until the meatballs are cooked through. Serve hot or as they cool to warm.

GREEN PEA, TARRAGON & GOAT'S CHEESE FRITTATA
SERVES 1

A real frittata isn't a quiche without pastry, it's an omelette. A thin, just cooked, glorious thing: if it isn't eaten straightaway, never refrigerate it lest it loose its eggy magic. It's here that some really nice peas come to the fore—in fact, I often just fry uncooked fresh peas in the oil until they change colour, but that only works with farm-fresh, young, sweet peas (or frozen ones, strangely). You need good free-range eggs and quality cheese to make it really sing.

> 3 eggs
> 1 tablespoon grated Italian-style parmesan cheese
>   (we like to use Grana Padano, but you could use a local
>   hard grating cheese that isn't too sharp)
> 2 teaspoons extra virgin olive oil
> 1 tablespoon green peas (frozen are okay in a pinch)
> 1 teaspoon roughly chopped French tarragon
> 2 tablespoons fresh goat's curd, or similar

Use a fork to whisk the eggs with the parmesan, salt and freshly milled black pepper. (Using a whisk gives a different end result.) Stir in 2 teaspoons of water. Preheat a griller (broiler) to full heat. Heat the oil in a medium frying pan over moderately high heat and fry the peas just for a minute or so with the tarragon, just to warm through, tossing every now and then until the peas have softened. Stir in the eggs, rubbing the bottom of the pan with the back of a fork so the eggs don't burn, just as you do an omelette. When nearly set, plop in teaspoonfuls of the goat's curd and place the pan under the griller to set the top. Serve straightaway.

NETTLE & FETA FILO PIE

SERVES 4–6

We have the occasional early summer flourish of stinging nettles, and find comfort knowing that eating nettles is our way to clean up the paddocks. But don't worry if you don't have them, because any decent green—such as silverbeet (Swiss chard) or a mixture—can work well too. I've used home-made filo because it's just so different to the commercial stuff—sturdy and earthier, albeit without the finesse—but you can use ready-made pastry.

6–8 handfuls fresh nettle leaves, stalks removed, well washed (about 1 cup blanched)

1 leek, green part only, washed and finely sliced

1–2 tablespoons extra virgin olive oil

4 tablespoons coarsely chopped dill

100 g (3½ oz) good-quality feta cheese, diced or crumbled

200 g (7 oz) fresh ricotta cheese (page 37)

4 eggs

lemon wedges, for serving

Filo pastry

250 g (9 oz/nearly 2 cups) plain (all-purpose) flour, plus extra for dusting

110 ml (3¾ fl oz) warm water

1 egg, lightly beaten

½ teaspoon salt

about ½ cup extra virgin olive oil

Throw the nettles into a big pot with the lid on and wilt them over low heat; the water left after washing will help them steam. Let them cool, then squeeze vigorously to remove all the liquid.

To make the filo pastry, mix all the ingredients except the oil together to make a dough. Knead for 4–5 minutes to a smooth texture. Wrap in plastic wrap and refrigerate for about an hour before rolling. Using a generous amount of flour and a big rolling pin, roll out the dough to a 40 x 80 cm (16 x 32 inch) rectangle. Cut into 8 equal squares (don't worry if they're not perfectly shaped), brush oil liberally on each, stack them on top of each other (ensuring the top isn't oiled, but rather floured), and roll this out to make an evenly thick piece of pastry 40 cm (16 inches) square.

Fry the leek well in 1 tablespoon of olive oil until soft, but not brown, and put it in a medium bowl with the nettles and the dill. Add the feta, ricotta, a generous pinch of salt and a good few grinds of black pepper. Mix well, then stir in the eggs.

Preheat the oven to 200°C (400°F). Make the pie by laying the pastry into a greased 30 cm (12 inch) pie dish lined with baking paper, or you could do it more free-form by using a baking tray. Place the filling in the middle and spread it out a little so there's enough pastry to bring up over the top to form the pie. Brush the top generously with more olive oil. Bake for 20–25 minutes until golden brown. Cool in the dish. Serve at room temperature with lemon wedges.

It's time to get our revenge on the nettles,

those usurpers in some parts of the paddocks.

What better justice, than baked in a pie?

SOFT PORK TACOS WITH TOMATILLO SALSA & CORIANDER

SERVES 8

I was lucky enough to get home-made fresh corn tortillas from a local mob, who sell tacos at markets. The real things are incomparable, so try to cadge some from your local food truck or real Mexican restaurant. In their absence, white corn tortillas are available at most supermarkets these days, so give them a go instead.

1.5 kg (3 lb 5 oz) boneless pork
   shoulder
2 teaspoons salt
2 teaspoons ground cumin
2 teaspoons ground coriander
   seeds
¼ teaspoon ground cloves
2 teaspoons ground chipotle
   powder (or substitute smoked
   sweet paprika)
8 garlic cloves, crushed
1 brown onion, peeled and sliced
500 ml (17 fl oz/2 cups) water

24 corn tortillas
coriander (cilantro) leaves,
   for serving
chilli sauce or pepper rum, or both

Roast tomatillo salsa
1 kg (2 lb 4 oz) tomatillos
5 large garlic cloves, peeled
4–5 long red chillies
½ cup (about a bunch) chopped
   coriander (cilantro)
3–4 tablespoons chopped red
   (Spanish) onion

Preheat the oven to 140°C (275°F).

Rub the pork shoulder all over with the salt, spices and garlic. Place the sliced onion in a medium ovenproof pot that has a tight-fitting lid, plop the pork on top, add the water, put on the lid and place in the oven for 4 hours or until falling apart. Check towards the end to make sure the water hasn't all evaporated; you want just a tiny bit of juice so the bottom doesn't burn.

Remove from the oven, allow to cool until it can be handled, and shred the pork with your hands, discarding any connective tissue or skin. Massage in any fat and cooking juices, and rub in the onion, too, which should be soft enough to fall apart. The meat should be a bit juicy and nicely spiced. Taste and add more salt or spice if need be. (This recipe makes plenty of pork for tacos for another day as well. If you want, you can use any cooked pork and simply simmer in the spices and garlic later to give it flavour, but doing it from scratch gives the best result.)

To make the salsa, roast the tomatillos in a roasting tin in a super-hot oven until they start to blacken and blister. They should be falling to bits. You can drain off excess juice after a few minutes and use this in your black beans (page 78) if you like. (It's really good.) In a separate pan, roast the garlic and chillies the same way, taking care not to darken the garlic too much or it will go acrid. The chillies can get quite a good dark colour without a problem, although it's optional whether you peel the charred skin off or not.

Drain any excess runny juice from the tomatillos and keep for other things (you'll need a bit for the salsa so it's not too dry). In a food processor, mix the tomatillo pulp, chillies and garlic, adding a touch of salt to taste. (If you want to freeze the tomatillo salsa base for later, do that now.) Stir through the coriander and onion, then serve at room temperature.

To serve, warm the tacos by dry frying in a hot frying pan, turning twice, until soft. Keep warm in a stack under a moist tea towel (dish towel) on a warm plate.

Serve the tortillas with the pork, salsa, perhaps some chilli sauce, and don't—whatever you do—put grated cheddar cheese or sour cream on the table.

▼ ▼

Tomatillos are a strange fruit, more closely related to a Cape gooseberry than a tomato. They are green and interesting to eat only after roasting or charring, becoming fragrant, nicely acidic and slightly sweet. They are one of the fruits we've managed to grow very successfully from the outset in our summer garden; we wait excitedly for each year's harvest, freezing excess salsa base for winter. In their absence, you can try to use green tomatoes, but the result will leave you feeling gypped if you've ever had the real thing.

BRAISED MEXICAN-STYLE BLACK BEANS WITH AVOCADO SALSA

SERVES 5–6

Sometimes, a plate of black beans is all the dinner you need. This version, with the slight richness of the avocado and egg salsa, makes our summer evenings quite often.

1 large brown onion, diced
2 garlic cloves, chopped
olive oil, for frying
1 cinnamon stick
1 teaspoon ground cumin, plus extra for serving (optional)
½ teaspoon ground coriander seeds
1 teaspoon chipotle powder (or substitute smoked sweet paprika)
3 cups black turtle beans, ideally soaked overnight
rice, natural yoghurt and coriander (cilantro) leaves, for serving

Avocado salsa
1 avocado, diced
1 hard-boiled egg, peeled and diced
a good handful of coriander (cilantro) leaves, chopped
2 tablespoons finely chopped spring onion (scallion) or red (Spanish) onion
about 1 teaspoon white wine vinegar
few squirts of Tabasco sauce

Heat a cast-iron pot that has a lid over medium heat and gently sauté the onion and garlic in olive oil until soft. Add all the spices and cook until fragrant, about a minute or two. Pop in the drained beans and cover with water. Bring to a boil then reduce the heat, cover and simmer, stirring occasionally, until beans are tender. They should take about 40 minutes if they've been soaked. (If you haven't soaked the beans, they'll take longer to cook and may cook slightly unevenly, but don't fret, they'll still taste good.) Add a little more water if the beans start to dry out, but you don't want much liquid left when they are cooked. Make sure you test three or four beans as sometimes one can be soft and the rest not at all ready.

Meanwhile, make the avocado salsa: mix all the ingredients, adding salt and pepper to taste.

Serve the beans with rice, salsa and a big dollop of natural yoghurt. Sprinkle with a little extra ground cumin if you wish and top with coriander leaves.

WATERMELON WITH CHILLI & LIME

SERVES A BIG CROWD

The combination of sweet, juicy watermelon with spice is intoxicating. You can do this with soy sauce in place of the salt, or replace the watermelon with pineapple.

1 whole watermelon
8–10 small dried chillies, roasted and ground
flaky salt, for serving
lime wedges, for serving

Cut the watermelon into wedges and then slices. Serve with the chilli and salt for dipping or sprinkling, and the lime for squeezing. And be sure to have a little beer on hand for those who like to partake.

SPINACH & RICOTTA GNOCCHI

SERVES 6

The amount of flour you'll need in these gnocchi depends a bit on your
ricotta and the spinach. Less moisture in both means less flour. Start with
100 g (3½ oz) and test one dumpling to see how it holds together. While it
may be more annoying to have to roll and cook them gently, soft gnocchi also
taste better, so less flour is more desirable.

750 g (1 lb 10 oz) well-wilted English spinach (frozen works fine),
   silverbeet (Swiss chard) leaves, or similar
500 g (1 lb 2 oz) fresh ricotta cheese (page 37), well drained
generous pinch of ground nutmeg
4 eggs
100–150 g (3½–5½ oz/⅔–1 cup) plain (all-purpose) flour,
   plus more for dusting
200 g (7 oz) butter, melted
lots of parmesan cheese, finely grated
lemon wedges, for serving (optional)

Squeeze the spinach as hard as you can to remove the water (this includes the frozen
stuff; just thaw it first).

Chop the spinach finely and mix well with the ricotta. When ready to start
cooking, heat a big saucepan of water and season really well with salt. Season the
spinach mixture generously with salt, freshly milled black pepper and nutmeg,
stir the eggs through until well muddled up, then fold through the flour.

Have a generous amount of extra flour in a bowl ready for rolling the gnocchi.
Take a good tablespoon or so of spinach mixture at a time and roll it between well-
floured palms, pressing to make a nice football-shaped dumpling. Dip this ball into
the flour to coat it well all over and lay on a tray to one side. Test this first gnoccho
by simmering in the water until it floats. If it holds together, there's enough flour, but
taste it to see if it needs more salt, pepper or nutmeg. When you're happy, continue
making dumplings until all the spinach mix is used up.

Make sure the big pot of cooking water is boiling, then cook in about 3–4 batches
by dropping the balls gently into the water. They will rise to the top when cooked.
Don't boil the water too vigorously or the gnocchi may fall apart.

Gently scoop out the gnocchi, drain well and place straight onto the serving
plates. Heat the butter to make it go nut brown, sprinkle the gnocchi with loads of
parmesan and pour the butter over. Serve with a pepper grinder on the table, some
more grated parmesan (and a lemon wedge, I find, is a nice touch, too).

CHARGRILLED ZUCCHINI & BUFFALO MOZZARELLA LASAGNE USING STALE CRUSTY BREAD

SERVES 4 OR SO

I make this with whatever cheese I have on hand: sometimes goat's curd; sometimes a fresh, sweet cow's ricotta, but always with good bread, oil and tomato.

> 2 tablespoons extra virgin olive oil, plus extra for drizzling
> 1 onion, diced
> 2 garlic cloves, crushed
> 500 ml (17 fl oz/2 cups) tomato passata (puréed tomatoes)
> 1–3 basil leaves, torn
> half a loaf rustic (sourdough, chewy) stale bread
> extra virgin olive oil
> 6 zucchini (courgettes), sliced lengthways, chargrilled
> 300 g (10½ oz) buffalo mozzarella
> about 50 g (1¾ oz) parmesan cheese, grated

Preheat the oven to 180°C (350°F).

Heat the oil in a medium saucepan over modest heat and fry the onion for about 5 minutes until soft. Add the garlic and cook another couple of minutes. Stir in the tomato passata and bring to the boil. Simmer for 10 minutes, adding a torn basil leaf or three.

Cut the bread into long slices. Oil a 2 litre (70 fl oz/8 cup) casserole dish, or similar, and cover the base with one-third of the sliced bread. Spoon over enough tomato sauce to soak in a bit, lay down one-third of the zucchini, then tear the mozzarella into small bits and dot over the zucchini, using about a third for each layer. Season well with salt and freshly milled black pepper and perhaps add a drizzle more oil. Repeat the layering until all the bread is used up. You could make more layers, but you really want to make sure there's enough tomato sauce left to moisten the top and enough mozzarella left to dot the top as well. Sprinkle the parmesan over the top and bake for 20–30 minutes until the top is nicely browned. Serve with a mixed green leaf salad.

THE BEST POACHED CHICKEN
(AND SOME GREAT STOCK FROM IT)
SERVES 4–6

A good poached chicken is simply a lovely way to celebrate the season (for a fancy use, see Poached Chicken, Shiitake and Sesame Salad on page 146). In this recipe, which I stumbled across while trying to replicate a Colombian stew (without actually having been there, or doing any proper research…), the corn adds sweetness to the broth, and tastes fantastic on its own or cut from the cob and added back to the broth to make a soup.

1.6 kg (3 lb 8 oz/no. 16) chicken, washed well
4 litres (140 fl oz/16 cups) water
1 tablespoon salt
stalks from 1 bunch coriander (cilantro), washed well
top half of half a bunch of spring onions (scallions)
2 corncobs, husks removed, each cut into 3 pieces

Put the chicken in a really big stockpot with all of the other ingredients and bring to the boil. Skim, turn down the heat and simmer for 15 minutes. Pop a lid on top, turn off the heat and allow the chicken to stand in the hot liquid for 1 hour. After an hour, cool by placing the pot base in cold water. Remove the chicken when cool enough to handle and shred the meat by hand, or cut it into pieces. Discard the bones and skin. Strain the broth and keep as stock for other uses.

SOUTH INDIAN-INSPIRED FISH & EGGPLANT CURRY

SERVES 4

A warm night, a subtle curry. The sweetness of good fish and the creaminess of long-cooked eggplant. What's not to like?

1 large eggplant (aubergine)
2 tablespoons vegetable oil or ghee
½ red (Spanish) onion, grated
  or puréed
a man's thumb worth of ginger,
  finely grated
6 garlic cloves, grated
1 long green chilli, finely sliced
  (or to taste)
½ teaspoon salt
1 tablespoon black mustard seeds

1 teaspoon ground turmeric
400 ml (14 fl oz) coconut milk
  (rather than cream)
500 g (1 lb 2 oz) bluespot mullet,
  morwong, gurnard or similar
  pale-fleshed fish fillets (flathead
  would work reasonably well, too)
about 20 curry leaves
lime or lemon juice, to taste
steamed rice, for serving

Preheat the oven to 220°C (425°F). Prick the eggplant in a couple of places and put it, whole, on a baking tray. Bake for about 20 minutes or until soft through. Remove and keep to one side.

In a heavy-based frying pan or saucepan, heat the oil over low heat and fry the onion, ginger, garlic and chilli with the salt for several minutes, stirring often, until it loses its really hot smell and becomes sweet and aromatic. This will happen before the mix goes brown, but don't worry if a little starts to colour up as you cook it. Add more oil while it cooks if it seems a bit dry.

Tip in the mustard seeds and continue frying until they make a gentle popping sound. Add the turmeric and fry, stirring constantly, for another 30 seconds.

Slosh in the coconut milk, crank up the heat, stir so there are no bits stuck to the pan, and turn down to a simmer for 5 minutes. At this point the sauce is just about done so you can turn it off and do other things for a while if you like.

The eggplant should be cool enough to handle by now, so peel off the skin and discard it. Chop the silken flesh into bite-size chunks. Skin the fish if you can, and cut the flesh into decent-size bits that are more than a mouthful (it'll flake apart easily after it's cooked).

Reheat the sauce, throw in the curry leaves and squeeze in a little lime or lemon juice. Taste for seasoning (it will probably need a tiny bit more salt), then add the eggplant and simmer for 2 minutes. Plop the fish into the sauce, making sure it's all covered, and simmer until it's just heated through and hence just cooked.

Serve with steamed rice.

GRILLED TROUT STUFFED WITH SHEEP'S SORREL & TOMATO BAY SAUCE

SERVES 4

Good fish cooked on the bone needs little except for a bit of acid (here from the lemony flavour of sheep's sorrel, a fiddle-shaped weed we find in our garden; substitute regular sorrel if you're not sure what sheep's sorrel is). I've dressed it up with the buttery, toasty flavour of pine nuts and a bit of fresh-tasting tomato sauce.

3 tablespoons extra virgin olive oil
1 bay leaf
150 ml (5 fl oz) tomato passata (puréed tomatoes)
4 fresh trout
a good handful of sheep's sorrel or other sorrel,
    or even a few thin slices of lemon
50 g (1¾ oz) pine nuts, lightly toasted, for serving

Heat 2 tablespoons of the olive oil in a frying pan and add the bay leaf and tomato passata. Cook gently for 5 minutes to release the flavour of the bay into the sauce. Set aside until ready to cook the fish.

To grill the fish, simply lay a few sorrel leaves inside the cavity of each one. Brush well with olive oil and season with salt inside and out. I like black pepper, too, but not everybody does with fish. Place in a fish grill, or similar (or simply barbecue or pan fry), cooking for about 3–4 minutes on each side, depending on the heat. You can check if cooked by gently pressing the flesh. When done, the fish will flake under your finger at the fattest part.

Serve the fish with the tomato sauce and pine nuts to one side, perhaps with a plate for the bones if you're inside.

CHAPTER

3

BARBECUE

I do like a fire. And the way it does things to meats, to seafood, to anything you cook over it or in it. Problem is that summer can mean total fire bans and a heightened fire risk. Luckily, we have options, like a gas barbecue, and a safe little fire can produce food with just as much flavour as a big one.

Think oregano and mint-scented mixed meat cevapcici, cooked over coals. Or whole fish, smoky from the grill. Use the barbecue to take sweet, tender lamb chops to the next level, or to add a mouth-watering charred flavour to zucchini and more.

A good barbecue may be nothing more than a few sticks and some flame, burning to coals. But even the gas barbecue does a remarkable job of fuelling the appetite, browning the meats and keeping any excess heat out of the house.

FLATHEAD TACOS

SERVES 4

This is a great, messy, spicy dish that is suited well to the barbecue and outdoor eating. Soft tortillas encase spiced fish and a lively pico de gallo salsa (which means 'rooster's beak', but is really just a fresh salsa with as many variations as there are cooks).

600 g (1 lb 5 oz) flathead fillets
    or other firm white fish,
    cut into 2 cm (¾ inch) dice
3 tablespoons olive oil
juice of 1 lime
20 soft white corn tortillas,
    10 cm (4 inch) diameter

Salsa
2 garlic cloves, hit with the flat of
    a knife and skin discarded
1 green capsicum (pepper), seeded
    and finely diced
6 roma (plum) tomatoes, seeded
    and cut into 1 cm (⅜ inch) dice

1 small red (Spanish) onion,
    finely diced
1–2 small red or green chillies,
    finely sliced
6 coriander (cilantro) stalks,
    including roots, well washed
juice of 1 lime
2 tablespoons extra virgin olive oil

Fish spice
2 teaspoons fennel seeds
2 teaspoons coriander seeds
2 teaspoons cumin seeds
1–2 teaspoon chipotle powder
    or similar chilli powder

To make the salsa, combine the garlic, capsicum, tomato, onion and sliced chilli. Finely chop the coriander, including the roots. Add the half you chopped from the bottom end to the other ingredients and reserve the rest for later. Season with salt and freshly milled black pepper. Stir well and let stand for about half an hour.

Meanwhile, make the fish spice using a mortar and pestle to crush the combined fennel, coriander and cumin seeds with ¾ teaspoon salt until it forms a fine powder. Mix in the chipotle powder, scatter over the fish and toss coat the fish evenly.

When you're ready to eat, warm the tortillas by heating each one on the edge of the barbecue hotplate (or in a hot cast-iron pan) for a few seconds on each side and store in a folded clean tea towel (dish towel). The tortillas will stay warm and soft.

To finish the salsa, add 1 teaspoon of salt, some pepper, the lime juice, extra virgin olive oil and the reserved chopped coriander leaves to the salsa and stir just to mix it well.

Oil the centre of the barbecue hotplate and fry the fish, stirring often, until cooked through. When it has changed colour, it's cooked. As soon as it is ready, scoop from the hotplate into a warmed bowl and squeeze the lime juice over.

Lay all the ingredients on the table and let everybody help themselves. You make a taco by reclining a warm tortilla on your plate, topping with a little fish, plenty of salsa (avoiding the garlic cloves), and rolling it up. Perhaps put some hot chilli sauce on the table for heat lovers, too.

CHARGRILLED WHOLE LEATHERJACKET WITH GREEN SAUCE

SERVES 8

A delicious but underutilised fish, leatherjacket is best cooked on the bone. So a barbecue is the perfect place to cook it, especially in summer.

4–5 tablespoons chopped coriander (cilantro) leaves
juice of 1 lime
½ teaspoon ground cumin seeds
½ teaspoon sweet paprika
½ teaspoon salt
generous pinch of freshly milled black pepper
80 ml (2½ fl oz/⅓ cup) extra virgin olive oil, plus extra for brushing
8 small leatherjackets, or firm white fish, gutted

Preheat a barbecue or chargrill to high heat.

Mix the coriander, lime, cumin, paprika, salt, pepper and oil together. This is your green sauce.

Brush the fish with a little oil, and cut slits into each side if it's big, to help it cook evenly: more slits are needed at the fat end of the fish. Chargrill, turning to brown each side, until the fish is cooked but not too charred.

Serve warm, accompanied by the green sauce and more salt on the table for all those who need it.

BARBECUED LAMB WITH ZUCCHINI, MINT & FETA SALAD

SERVES 8

Who doesn't adore a wood-fired barbecue with lamb? To me, this dish just tastes of summer.

12 zucchini (courgettes), topped and tailed
olive oil, for rubbing
16 lamb cutlets
about 10 mint leaves, torn
100 g (3½ oz) feta cheese, crumbled
2 tablespoon extra virgin olive oil

Cut the zucchini into thin strips using a knife or, even better, a mandolin slicer. Rub them with the tiniest amount of olive oil and chargrill until lightly coloured on both sides. Leave to one side while you get the lamb on. Rub the lamb with a bit of oil, season well with salt and freshly milled black pepper, and grill on both sides until cooked to your liking.

While the lamb cooks, toss the zucchini with the mint and feta, the olive oil and enough salt and pepper to make it flavoursome: remember that the feta will have its own salt content that you'll need to take into account.

Serve the lamb with the salad.

ZUCCHINI FLOWER & BUFFALO MOZZARELLA PIZZA COOKED ON THE BARBECUE

MAKES 3–4 PIZZAS, ENOUGH FOR 3–4 PEOPLE

I fell in love with this pizza on a research trip to Italy in the 1990s. Ever since, I've been trying to recreate the flavours, and a super-hot barbecue with a lid is one of the best places to get high heat onto the crust. If you have a super-duper wood-fired oven, of course you'd use that.

extra virgin olive oil, for brushing
8 zucchini (courgette) flowers, cut into fine strips
2–3 whole buffalo mozzarella (allow 1 ball per pizza if you're generous), or try other cheeses
3–4 tablespoons pure cream (35% fat)

Pizza dough
270 g (9½ oz/scant 2 cups) plain (all-purpose) flour
7 g (¼ oz) sachet dried yeast
1 teaspoon salt
1 teaspoon sugar
200 ml (7 fl oz/about ¾ cup) water
olive oil, for drizzling

Make the dough a day or two ahead; it ensures virtually no kneading. To make the dough, mix the dry ingredients together. Make a well in the centre and pour in the water, mixing with a spoon until it's too hard to mix, then finish mixing with your hand to make a smoothish dough. Sprinkle in a little more flour at a time if needed. Form into a ball, rub all over with olive oil, pop into a bowl big enough so it can expand, cover with plastic wrap then stand in the fridge until ready to use: at least a couple of hours.

Preheat the barbecue with the lid down. For a communal experience, let each person make their own pizza. Roll out the dough—using a mist of flour and stretching it with your hands until it's the size you want—and lay it on a pizza tray: those ones with holes in are the best. Brush with enough extra virgin olive oil to make it glisten. Lay the zucchini flowers on the dough then tear the buffalo mozzarella into pieces and dot around. Season with a little salt and pepper, then drizzle a tiny bit of cream on top; no more than 1 tablespoon per pizza.

Roast, with the lid down, on the chargrill side of the barbecue if you have one, checking every couple of minutes. It will scorch on the bottom, without colouring so much on top. Turn it around and move it to a cooler part of the barbecue if it's darkening too much. It can take as little as 3–5 minutes, longer on some barbecues.

TWICE-COOKED PORK SHOULDER CHOPS WITH SOY & STAR ANISE
SERVES 6

Shoulder chops, sometimes called neck chops, come from my favourite part of the pig. The shoulder is flavoursome, breaks down to a great texture, and stays moist when cooked. I braise the chops first, then simply scorch them on the barbecue when it's time to eat. It seems like an unnecessary first step, but braising creates an even more delicious dish than marinating alone.

> 6 pork shoulder chops
> 3 litres (105 fl oz/12 cups) water
> 250 ml (9 fl oz/1 cup) soy sauce
> 4 whole star anise
> 1 cinnamon stick
> 1 teaspoon Chinese five spice
> 1 teaspoon sugar
> 1 tablespoon black vinegar (or use normal rice, apple cider
>   or wine vinegar if you don't have it)
> oil, for grilling or frying
> rice, noodles or boiled potatoes, for serving

Lay the chops in a saucepan that fits them snugly. Add all the other ingredients except the oil, put the pan over very high heat and bring to the boil. Turn the temperature right down and let the meat barely simmer for about 90 minutes or so. Allow the meat to cool in the liquid, ideally, then remove and drain well. You can make this ahead of time and leave it in the fridge for a couple of days before using.

When you're ready to eat, heat a barbecue hotplate or even a frying pan well over high heat, oiling very lightly. Sear the meat on each side to brown, taking care it doesn't burn. Because it's cooked, the meat simply needs to be reheated. Serve the pork with rice or noodles or even some spuds, and reserve the poaching liquid for noodle soups.

Summer means long days and short sleeps.

Wide brims and short pants.

CORN WITH SMOKED PAPRIKA, CORIANDER BUTTER

SERVES 6

A good sweet end-of-summer corncob just seems made to go with coriander. Here, I've jazzed it up with a little smoky paprika and chipotle (available from good spice shops).

6 super-fresh corncobs, in their husks
100 g (3½ oz) butter
2 teaspoons chipotle powder
½ teaspoon smoked paprika
½ teaspoon ground cumin
a few tablespoons chopped coriander (cilantro) leaves
limes, for squeezing

Peel the husk back from the corn, as you would peel a banana, and remove the silk (the fine stringy bits). Fold back the husks so the corn is protected from the fire.

Over some modest coals, using a grate, chargrill the corn until it starts to brown a bit. You can also do this on a hotplate, on which it is easier to control the heat, but it isn't quite as good in terms of the flavour. Turn the corn so it browns a bit on all sides; the kernels will be steaming in their own juices as the corn heats. Good corn will only need a bit of heating. Don't use old cobs.

Mash the butter with the spices and add a pinch of salt and then the coriander. Serve the corn with the butter, perhaps some more spice mix, and limes on the table.

HERBED CEVAPS

SERVES 10

Making sausages at home is often hindered by the lack of a machine or the lack of skins. Or both. Here is a very simple mix, inspired by Balkan sausages called cevapcici (which are often shortened to cevaps in that particular Australian way) that you can knock up as easily as you would a few patties. Be sure to keep things chilled for best results and if you want to alter the ratios of each type of meat to what you've got, feel free.

500 g (1 lb 2 oz) minced (ground) beef
500 g (1 lb 2 oz) minced (ground) pork
500 g (1 lb 2 oz) minced (ground) lamb
2 eggwhites
1 tablespoon salt
5 garlic cloves, crushed
3 teaspoons ground dried thyme
3 teaspoons ground dried mint
3 teaspoons ground dried oregano
½ teaspoon freshly milled black pepper
Yoghurt Flatbread (see page 215), for serving
natural yoghurt, for serving
coriander (cilantro) or mint leaves, for serving

Mix all of the ingredients well together with your hands, just until the mixture becomes sticky. Refrigerate for half an hour after making the mix. If using wooden skewers, soak them in water for at least 10 minutes to prevent them from burning during cooking.

Shape the mix by hand into sausage-like shapes, on skewers if using, then chargrill or barbecue on medium heat for a few minutes each side to cook through.

Serve with yoghurt flatbread, a dollop or two of natural yoghurt and some freshly torn coriander or mint leaves.

BACON & BAKED BEAN JAFFLES

SERVES 4

These jaffles (toasted sandwiches) don't have much butter on the bread because the bacon melts a bit of fat into the outside, too. The tricky part is trying to get the bacon out of the jaffle iron when the sandwich is cooked, as it can stick a bit. Lean bacon may not prove quite as successful as some good fatty stuff from older breed pigs; if you use the streaky end, then it should work fine.

4 rashers (slices) of bacon, cut to size of the jaffle iron
8 slices of bread
butter, for spreading (optional)
4–8 slices of cheddar cheese
about 8 tablespoons of baked beans

Line one side of a jaffle iron with the cut pieces from half a rasher of bacon. Pop a slice of bread on top (you may want to butter it lightly on the downward side). Top with a slice of the cheese, 2 tablespoons of the baked beans (add another slice of cheese to help it stick better if you like) and the other piece of bread, again buttering the outside if you think it needs it. Lay the cut pieces from half a rasher of bacon on top, close the jaffle iron and cook until well browned. Repeat three times with the remaining ingredients.

PAPRIKA-DUSTED MINUTE STEAK SANDWICH WITH HUMMUS & PARSLEY SALAD

SERVES 4

It's good to have a hot—but not too hot—barbecue to cook this, so the paprika sizzles without burning. That way you'll end up with a magnificent, lightly spiced sandwich that takes the usual steak sandwich to new heights.

¼ small red (Spanish) onion, finely diced

1 teaspoon ground sumac

¼ teaspoon ground cumin

8 slices of bread, ideally something like a ciabatta, or 4 bread rolls

1 tablespoon pomegranate molasses

1 tablespoon extra virgin olive oil

2 large handfuls of flat-leaf (Italian) parsley leaves, washed
    and dried well

4 minute steaks, 150 g (5½ oz) each, from the top end of the rump

about 2 teaspoons paprika

olive oil, for cooking

about ⅓ cup Hummus (see page 64)

Mix the onion with a pinch of salt, the sumac and cumin and set aside for 5 minutes. When you're ready to eat, heat the barbecue under a flatiron plate, or heat a pan over medium–high heat. Pop the bread or buns on one side of the barbecue to warm lightly.

Mix the onion with the pomegranate molasses and extra virgin olive oil, add the parsley then toss this salad, seasoning with a little extra salt, if need be. Put the steaks on a large plate. Sprinkle the paprika on the steaks evenly, drizzle a little oil over and waggle the steaks around so they're lightly oiled all over. Season with salt and pepper and cook for about 1 minute on each side to sear but not burn the paprika.

Spread the hummus on the bread, lay each steak on a slice and add the salad to the top. Cover with another slice of bread and chomp down with slightly greasy fingers and a good beer to one side.

BAKED PORK & FENNEL SAUSAGES WITH GRAPES, OLIVES & BAY

SERVES 4–6

This is a rustic, delicious dish of sausages simply cooked in the oven with a few other flavours, including sour green grapes. The best sausages to use are pure pork ones, with no starch added and using coarsely ground meat, in the southern French or Italian style.

2–3 tablespoons olive oil
4 bay leaves, fresh if possible
4–5 thyme sprigs
50 g (1¾ oz) black olives
1 kg (2 lb 4 oz) pork and fennel sausages, or similar
200 g (7 oz) unripe green grapes

Heat the oil in a large, preferably heavy-based frying pan then add the bay leaves and thyme. Pop in the black olives, sausages and grapes. Nestle the pan into the side of a fire (or you could do it on a stove top on medium heat) and cook the sausages for about 10 minutes, turning often, or until they start to colour and are cooked through. The grapes may explode, which is fine. The only thing to do is to make sure nothing burns and the sausages aren't raw, really.

Serve hot with bread, spuds or even polenta.

SAGANAKI WITH SMOKY EGGPLANT PURÉE & POMEGRANATE DRESSING

SERVES 6 AS A STARTER OR SNACK

In this dish, simple fried cheese (which is the saganaki bit) gets a lively dose of unctuousness from smoked eggplant, and the sprightliness of pomegranate in the dressing. The baba ghanoush is a smoky eggplant purée that is amazing with flatbread and even better with the fried haloumi and pomegranate dressing. If you can get hold of fresh pomegranates, lucky you, especially because they're usually not available until autumn where we live. Simply scatter some pink pearls over the dish with the herbs.

400 g (14 oz) haloumi cheese,
cut into slices
olive oil, for frying
2 tablespoons extra virgin olive oil
2 tablespoons pomegranate
molasses
handful of flat-leaf (Italian) parsley
8 or so mint leaves
2 tablespoons pine nuts,
lightly toasted
lemon wedges (optional) and
bread, for serving

Baba ghanoush

2 large eggplants (aubergines),
about 1 kg (2 lb 4 oz) in total
3–4 garlic cloves, crushed
2 tablespoons tahini (sesame
seed paste)
1 tablespoon Greek-style yoghurt
1–2 tablespoons lemon juice,
or to taste
1–2 tablespoons extra virgin
olive oil
1 teaspoon salt, or to taste
¼ teaspoon freshly milled
black pepper

To make the baba ghanoush, grill the eggplants over coals or a hotplate until the skin has blackened and the inside is very soft. (You can control the smokiness by darkening the eggplant only slightly and finishing off roasting in the oven.) I sometimes smoke my eggplants by scorching the outside on a gas burner then finish them in the oven.

Allow to cool, then peel off the skin. Rubbing with paper towel then scraping with a knife is the best way, I find. Blitz the flesh with the remaining ingredients in a food processor, then taste and add extra salt and lemon juice if needed.

Rinse the haloumi or soak if too salty, then drain and pat dry. Heat a little oil in a large frying pan over medium heat until hot, then fry the haloumi slices on each side until well browned.

While it cooks, spread the baba ghanoush over the platter or plate, about 1 cm (⅜ inch) thick. Lay the cooked haloumi slices over the top. Mix the extra virgin olive oil with the pomegranate molasses and drizzle over the top. Scatter the parsley and mint over the lot along with the pine nuts and serve with bread and lemon wedges on the table. The baba ghanoush also goes brilliantly with duck.

SALADS +SOUPS

Soup seems a strange beast to eat when it's hot outside. But, like drinking tea in the tropics, a warm yet liquid meal can be a salve for summer days. Corn and coriander soup almost leaves you lighter than before you ate it. And while pea and ham soup might be a winter staple, the summer version, using fresh peas, is easy on the lips and gentle on the tummy.

A salad could be the entire meal, too. We like to sear a little albacore tuna to use in a substantial salad. Or shred some roasted or confited duck. A decent salad may have cheese, or nuts, and become more than just a bowl of chlorophyll and lemon juice. Something with enough substance to call itself lunch, or dinner. Or both.

While summer fruits are high on the menu, I'm someone who tends to avoid fruit in my salads, so the watermelon version we give here is a revelation. The salty tang of the feta and the hint of spice from chilli is just enough to turn this from dessert firmly into the savoury camp. And let's not forget chicken. A poached chicken (where the poaching liquid can become your stock for your next day's soup) is pretty divine when given a few shiitakes for company.

ALBACORE TUNA, TOMATO & CUCUMBER SALAD WITH DILL & OLIVES

SERVES 8

Albacore is fished more sustainably than most other tuna and it eats really well. You usually have to preorder it from your fishmonger, but it's worth it. Well handled, it's delicious for everything from a tuna sashimi to this salad.

500 g (1 lb 2 oz) albacore tuna fillet in a log shape
olive oil, for rubbing
2 telegraph (long) cucumbers
10 ripe cherry tomatoes, or equivalent
half a bunch of dill, torn into small sprigs
100 g (3½ oz) black olives
1 tablespoon lemon juice
3 tablespoons extra virgin olive oil

Rub the tuna with the olive oil and season well with salt and pepper. Only the outside is seasoned at this stage, so you can be more generous than usual.

Heat a chargrill pan or barbecue to very hot and sear the tuna on all sides. Allow it to cool then slice about 5 mm (¼ inch) thick.

Chop the cucumbers into roughly bite-size bits and put them in a big bowl with the tuna and tomatoes. Add the dill, olives, lemon juice and olive oil and toss gently to combine. You'll need to add bit more salt and pepper now.

Serve with good bread and olive oil for drizzling.

A VERY GOOD GREEK SALAD

SERVES 6

Most pitted black olives aren't very nice. Partly that's because they are actually green olives that are put through a pitting machine (black ones are too ripe) before being dyed to please the eye, rather than the palate. A good Greek salad should only celebrate the best of the season and the pantry, and so avoids such abominations.

1 small red (Spanish) onion, finely sliced
½ teaspoon salt
½ teaspoon sugar
4–5 very ripe tomatoes, diced
2 telegraph (long) cucumbers, cut into chunks
2–3 tablespoons chopped flat-leaf (Italian) parsley
100 g (3½ oz) black olives, rinsed
2 tablespoons lemon juice
4 tablespoons extra virgin olive oil, or slightly more
150 g (5½ oz) good-quality feta, diced

Pop the onion into a big bowl with the salt and sugar and toss to combine, then allow to stand for 15–20 minutes. This will soften the onion's potency somewhat.

In the same bowl, toss the onion (and the juice that will come out) with the tomatoes, cucumber, parsley and olives, using your fingertips to make sure it's mixing well. Add a little pepper, plus the lemon juice and olive oil, and toss a little more. At the last minute, mix through the feta and serve immediately with a glass of something summery, some good bread and perhaps a bit of meat or veg hot off the chargrill.

FAT PIG'S PANZANELLA

SERVES 4

My panzanella (tomato and bread salad) is loosely based on a Tuscan dish that relies on wet, ripe tomatoes. If your tomatoes are a bit sharp, you may want to add a good pinch of sugar to balance the flavours somewhat.

750 g (1 lb 10 oz) ripe tomatoes, chopped
1 garlic clove, finely chopped or crushed
about 15 basil leaves, torn
1 small red (Spanish) onion, finely diced
250 g (9 oz) crusty, stale white bread (preferably wood-fired;
    a ciabatta works well)
1 tablespoon red wine vinegar
4 tablespoons extra virgin olive oil
about 20 small white anchovies, or similar (use parmesan cheese
    or olives in their place if you don't like anchovies)

Put the chopped tomatoes in a bowl and salt them well. Add the garlic, basil and onion and leave to stand for an hour. Tear the bread into smallish pieces and splash it with the vinegar. Mash the tomatoes up a bit with your hands and add the bread. If the mixture is not wet enough, add more tomatoes, or you could sprinkle in a little water or some good passata (tomato purée). Tip most of the olive oil over the salad, taste and add salt and pepper if needed. Scatter the anchovies around—perhaps leaving some on the table for those who like to make it really sing—and serve immediately, perhaps with a little more oil on top.

▼ ▼

I know you don't have time for this, but it's important. There are these two farmers having a beer in a pub, right. The elder, wiser, wealthier farmer has been growing tomatoes for 30 years. His mate, who's been growing a mixture of vegetables, wants to achieve the same success as his elder, and is very keen to know which type of tomato to grow. Looking up from The Land, *and peering over his reading glasses, the older bloke sums up his mate. 'What type of tomato depends,' he answers, in that long, slow Aussie drawl designed for maximum efficiency (and to keep the flies out). 'It depends on whether you want to sell the tomatoes, or eat them.'*

LENTIL & PARSLEY SALAD WITH SHREDDED DUCK & DUCK CRACKLING

SERVES 4 AS A STARTER

I adore the richness of the duck, the earthiness of the lentils and the sweetness of walnut oil, cut by slivers of radish and a sharp lettuce. Little bits of torn radicchio are a nice touch, too, and if you've got some duck roasting juices, you can add them to the lentil cooking water as well.

> 1 tablespoon olive oil
> ½ small red (Spanish) onion, finely chopped
> 100 g (3½ oz) small green lentils
> 1 bay leaf
> 2 slow-roasted duck legs, flesh stripped from the bone
>   and shredded with your fingers, skin reserved
> 1–2 red radishes, finely sliced
> handful mizuna leaves, or use frisée (curly endive)
> small handful flat-leaf (Italian) parsley leaves
> 1 tablespoon balsamic or other mild vinegar
> 2 tablespoons walnut or extra virgin olive oil
> ¼ teaspoon salt

Heat the oil in a medium saucepan over low heat and fry the onion well until soft. Add the lentils, and just enough water to cover by 5 mm (¼ inch). Throw in the bay leaf and turn up the heat to get it to boil. Turn down to a simmer, cover, and keep an eye on the water so the lentils cook through but don't dry out: about 25–30 minutes. You want to get the cooking juices absorbed into the lentils by the time they're cooked. Add salt and pepper a few minutes before taking from the stove. When cooked, set aside in the pan and remove the bay leaf.

When ready to serve, warm the duck slightly. Mix the warmed duck with the radish, mizuna and parsley and toss to combine.

Whisk the balsamic vinegar, oil, salt and some freshly ground black pepper together until well combined. Dress the lentils with half the dressing and toss to moisten. Gently add the duck mixture with the remaining dressing and mix with your fingertips. Serve immediately.

The duck skin from the slow-cooked legs can be salted and crisped in a pan and added to the salad at the last minute. It's kind of like duck crackling.

APPLE & RADISH SALAD
WITH WALNUT OIL

SERVES 4 AS A SIDE DISH

The heat of radishes goes really well with the sweet tartness of apple.
Mix them and you've got a perfect end-of-summer (or autumn) salad.
This salad is amazing with cloth-bound cheddar such as one from
Pyengana Dairy Company, or other firm, aged cheese.

handful of mixed salad leaves, well washed and dried
4–5 radishes, washed and cut into eighths (you can finely slice one
for garnishing)
2 apples, peeled and cut into bite-size bits
juice of ½ lemon
2 teaspoons sherry vinegar
1 tablespoon walnut oil
1 teaspoon olive oil
lovage, or young celery leaves, for garnishing

Tear the salad leaves if too big, and discard any long stems. Toss gently with the
radishes and apple. Mix the lemon juice and sherry vinegar with the combined
oils and season well with salt and pepper to taste. Splash the dressing over the salad
and toss to coat, throwing in the lovage or celery leaves at the last minute.

Wallows and watering and wheelbarrows.

A battle of us against the sun and the breeze.

PEAR, WALNUT & CHEDDAR SALAD

SERVES 6

While I don't always love fruit in salad, a little pear is always a nice thing when matched with a bit of sharp cheese. Add the snap of top-notch walnuts and the crisp, lightly bitter radish, and you've nearly got a meal in one dish.

    ¼ small cabbage, finely shredded
    2 pears, finely sliced
    100 g (3½ oz) walnut pieces
    3–4 radishes, finely sliced
    handful of flat-leaf (Italian) parsley leaves, torn
    2 tablespoons lemon juice
    2 tablespoons walnut oil, or other nut oil such as hazelnut
    100 g (3½ oz) good old cheddar cheese, finely shredded with
        a potato peeler, or similar

Mix the cabbage and pears with the walnuts, radish slices and parsley. Dress the salad with the lemon juice and oil, and season with salt and pepper. Use your fingers to gently toss the salad and coat it evenly in the dressing, then finally add the cheese, and give a little last toss. Serve as a light lunch, with bread, or as part of a picnic or barbecue meal.

SMOKED TROUT, EGG & PICKLED CABBAGE SALAD

SERVES 6

I adore this kind of salad, where the warmth of smoked fish is paired with the simplicity of boiled potatoes, the richness of egg and the acidity of some pickled cabbage. When the potatoes are cooked, it's good to work fast so you have a lightly warm salad by the end. If it goes cold that won't matter; it'll still taste terrific.

500 g (1 lb 2 oz) baby pink eye potatoes (or other small, new waxy potatoes), halved and boiled until just cooked
1 teaspoon dill seeds
2 smoked trout fillets, flaked
2–3 tablespoons coarsely chopped dill
4–5 tablespoons Meyer Mayonnaise (see page 55)
6 hard-boiled eggs, halved
extra virgin olive oil, for serving

Pickled cabbage
¼ red cabbage
1 teaspoon salt
2 tablespoons white wine vinegar

To make the pickled cabbage, toss the chopped or sliced cabbage in a little salt and massage well with your fingers to gently break down the flesh. Add the vinegar and toss again, then set aside to pickle for about 3 hours before using.

To make the salad, toss the potatoes with the pickled cabbage and dill seeds. Gently fold through the flaked trout and chopped dill, then dress on plates with the hard-boiled eggs around. Add a good dollop of meyer mayonnaise. Serve with a bit of freshly milled pepper on top, and perhaps a drizzle of olive oil.

SUMMER PEA & HAM SOUP

SERVES 6

This is a delightfully runny version of an unstirred risotto, based loosely on Venice's risi e bisi (page 52). It's perfect for summer when you can kick back and let the whole thing simmer. It's also fine for cheats, as it's okay to use frozen peas and that smoky leg ham you spirited away after the glut of Christmas for another day.

80 g (2¾ oz) butter
1 leek, pale parts only, finely chopped
200 g (7 oz) ham, finely diced
200 g (7 oz/about 1 cup) risotto rice
3 litres (105 fl oz/12 cups) chicken stock
400 g (14 oz) very fresh peas (or you could even use frozen baby peas)
50 g (1¾ oz) parmesan cheese, finely grated

Heat the butter in a large saucepan over medium heat and fry the leek gently, so you hear a faint hiss from the pan. Use a wooden paddle to move it around occasionally and continue frying for about 5 minutes until the leek is soft but not browned.

Add the ham and rice, then drown the lot in the stock. Season well. (Remember the ham will furnish the broth with some salt, and so will the cheese at the end.)

Bring to a boil then turn right down to a gurgle. Stir occasionally for 15–20 minutes until the rice is cooked through, depending on the brand of rice. Tip in the peas and bring back to the boil. Remove from the heat and stir in the cheese. Leave it to sit a couple of minutes (while you get the bowls and call out, 'Dinner'). Serve hot.

CHARGRILLED ZUCCHINI & MINT SALAD

SERVES 4–6

I do love a little charred zucchini, and it only takes a plant or two to satisfy our family's needs, they grow so vigorously. Here, the zucchini is given a lift using mint, to make it more fragrant. The size and heat of the chilli will depend on your tastes.

4 zucchini (courgettes)
2–3 tablespoons extra virgin olive oil
1 teaspoon sesame oil
1 red chilli, finely sliced
2 tablespoons shredded flat-leaf (Italian) parsley
2 tablespoons shredded Vietnamese mint
2 tablespoons shredded mint

Cut the zucchini lengthways into about 4 mm (⅛ inch) slices. Lightly brush with the olive oil, sprinkle with salt and freshly milled black pepper, and chargrill until lightly coloured and tender. Toss with the sesame oil, chilli and combined herbs. Serve warm or at room temperature.

ACQUACOTTA
(A HUMBLE SOUP WITH A NOBLE FLAVOUR)
SERVES 4

Acquacotta is one of the most unassuming soups: a filler for farm workers that didn't cost too much or need any meat or stock. This classic Italian soup (meaning, literally, 'cooked water') can use whatever you happen to have in the house. Really, it can be as simple or as complex as you like. My version is one of the most austere, relying on good bread, good tomato and great olive oil. If you don't have these—and some decent cheese—cook something else.

- 65 ml (2 fl oz/¼ cup) extra virgin olive oil
- 2 onions, chopped
- 2 large extremely ripe tomatoes, about 400 g (14 oz), chopped
  (you can get away with tinned rather than unripe fresh tomatoes)
- 1 litre (35 fl oz/4 cups) water
- about 1½ teaspoons salt
- 40 g (1½ oz) mild pecorino cheese, grated (or use Italian parmesan—
  a good cheddar could also work, but not as effortlessly)
- 4 eggs
- 4 thick slices of peasant-style bread
- 8 basil leaves, torn

Heat half the olive oil in large saucepan and fry the onion until nice and soft. Slop in the tomato, water, salt and freshly milled black pepper and simmer for a good 15 minutes.

Whisk the grated cheese and eggs together and season a little with pepper and possibly more salt.

Chargrill or toast the bread until it's dark but not burnt and place a slice each in the bottom of four large bowls. (Rub the bread with a raw garlic clove at this point, if you like.)

Add the basil to the boiling soup with the remaining olive oil, pour the egg mixture over the bread, and then ladle the soup over the top. It will cook the egg, melt the cheese a little and soak into the bread.

You may need to serve with a knife and fork if your bread is really resilient.

CUCUMBER & SESAME OIL SALAD

SERVES 6–8

This is a jazzed-up version of the cucumber salad we sometimes serve over summer. You can get away with just a little salt, rice vinegar and sesame oil, but the Sichuan pepper and black vinegar give it a little more zing for a change.

1 teaspoon Sichuan flowering peppercorns
2 teaspoons black vinegar
½ teaspoon sugar
½ teaspoon salt, or more to taste
1–2 tablespoons sesame oil
2 telegraph (long) cucumbers, peeled and cut into chunks
    (a roll-cut is ideal, if you know how to do it), seeded is optional

In a dry frying pan over medium heat, lightly toast the Sichuan pepper until it starts to change fragrance. You don't want to scorch it, just caramelise it a bit. Crush it lightly in a mortar and pestle.

Mix the vinegar, sugar and salt in a large bowl. Add the sesame oil and Sichuan pepper, then throw in the cucumber and toss to lightly coat.

Serve immediately as part of a Chinese-style meal, or at a barbecue with some twice-cooked pork (page 99) or the like.

From up high, you see the patchwork of colours,

from the lush green of the garden,

to the golden paddocks of high summer.

CAPONATA

MAKES ABOUT 1 KG (2 LB 4 OZ)

Okay, so it's not a salad. But what is it really? A relish? A pickle? It's an almost-salad, great for storing away for quick summer meals, for lifting barbecued meats or veg to new heights. Or for sneaking spoonfuls when you really should be doing the dishes or wiping the skirting boards.

3 large eggplants (aubergines), cut into cubes
1 teaspoon salt
roughly 500 ml (17 fl oz/2 cups) decent olive oil
1 brown onion, thinly sliced
4 celery stalks, finely chopped
4 tomatoes, peeled and diced
2 garlic cloves, finely chopped
1 tablespoon sugar
1 tablespoon red wine vinegar
2 tablespoons capers
90 g (3¼ oz/½ cup) green olives
65 g (2¼ oz/½ cup) toasted slivered almonds or pine nuts
generous handful of flat-leaf (Italian) parsley, coarsely chopped

Pop the eggplant into a large nonreactive bowl. Salt the eggplant lightly and leave to stand for about an hour. Drain well on paper towel.

Heat a very large frying pan over medium heat and fill with olive oil until it's about 1 cm (⅜ inch) deep.

Gently fry the eggplant until golden and soft. You may need to do this in two batches if your pan isn't big enough, adding more oil between batches if need be. Drain on paper towel and set aside.

Drain most of the oil from the pan, leaving about 2 mm (⅟₁₆ inch) in the base, and fry the onion and celery over medium heat until soft, then add tomatoes and garlic, season with salt and pepper and simmer for 15 minutes. Add sugar, vinegar, capers and green olives and cook for another 15 minutes. Turn off the heat, then stir through the eggplant, nuts and chopped parsley.

Caponata is best served at room temperature. A big jar of this in the fridge keeps for a week and is perfect to snack on with grilled sourdough bread and some cheese. Or with saganaki (page 110). Or as a condiment with fish.

WATERMELON, FETA & MINT SALAD
SERVES 4–6

The salty sting of feta and a pungent cold-pressed olive oil bring out a wonderful mouth-watering feel in this savoury salad. It's light, the melon is in season and the flavours snap you to attention without overwhelming anything else in the meal.

¼ small ripe watermelon, cut into 2 cm (¾ inch) cubes
200 g (7 oz) good feta cheese, such as Dodoni, cut into roughly
    5 mm (¼ inch) cubes or crumbled
about 10 mint leaves (or, even better, a mix of mint and basil)
1 small red (Spanish) onion, finely diced
1 tablespoon lime or lemon juice
3 tablespoons extra virgin olive oil
slivered fresh chilli (optional)

It's just a tossed salad. Put the watermelon and feta in a big bowl. The mint (or mint and basil) leaves should be shredded finely by stacking them up and cutting them crossways. Pop them in the same bowl as the watermelon, add the onion and give it all a bit of a toss. Throw in the lime juice (sprinkle to distribute it well) and the olive oil and plenty of freshly milled black pepper. A great olive oil will make all the difference. I like to add a few shreds of chilli sometimes, too. Mix it all up, and add a pinch or two of salt to bring out the flavours. Serve in the centre of the table with chargrilled or barbecued meats and crusty bread.

CORN & CORIANDER SOUP

SERVES 4–6

This soup is the best way to use the wonderful, summery, light broth you get from poaching a chook. You could jazz it up with a little crab meat and sesame oil, if you like.

> 1 quantity stock and the corncobs from The Best Poached Chicken
> (see page 84)
> 2 spring onions (scallions), finely sliced
> 1 bunch coriander (cilantro), coarsely chopped
> 1 lime, for squeezing

Trim the kernels from the corncobs by standing them on their ends and cutting down to the chopping board. Discard the cobs. Heat the stock in a large stockpot over high heat until simmering. Add the corn, and when it comes to the boil again, toss in the onion and coriander.

Serve the soup immediately, perhaps with bread to dip in, or even freshly steamed rice on the side, that you moisten in the soup spoon. Don't forget to put the lime on the table for squeezing into the soup.

CHICKEN & LIME SOUP
WITH CORN CHIPS
SERVES 8

This soup is very loosely based on the traditional Mexican sopa de lima.
It may look like a lot of ingredients, but most of them are spices and all
readily available. You can serve the soup in bowls and place the condiments
on the table so everyone can build their own soup. We tend to wait until
the end of summer to make it, when limes have dropped in price, because
they're an ingredient we definitely can't grow in our climes.

1.8 kg (4 lb/no.18) chicken
1 brown onion
4 garlic cloves, no need to peel
1 carrot
6 allspice berries
1 tablespoon salt
6 whole peppercorns
6 cloves
1 cinnamon stick
1 bunch coriander (cilantro)
1 onion, extra, peeled and
    cut into quarters

10 garlic cloves, unpeeled, extra
lime juice, for seasoning

To serve
mild fresh cheese (we used mild
    feta), crumbled or grated
1 avocado, peeled, cut into chunks
about 200 g (7 oz) good corn
    chips, not flavoured
3–4 limes, halved
chopped fresh chilli

Place the whole chicken in a large stockpot with the whole onion, garlic, whole carrot,
allspice, salt, peppercorns, cloves, cinnamon stick and the stalks and roots of the
coriander, then cover with water. Bring to a boil over high heat and then reduce
the heat, cover and simmer for an hour. Remove from the heat and allow to cool.

Once cool enough to handle, remove the chicken from the stock and strain,
reserving the liquid and discarding the vegetables and spices. Remove the chicken
meat from bones and shred. There will be plenty left over for sandwiches. Discard
the skin and carcass.

Grill (broil) the extra onion and garlic under high heat until soft and a little
charred on the edges. Discard the skin from the garlic. Put the onion and garlic in a
small food processor with a cup or so of the chicken stock and process into a paste.
Bring the chicken stock back to the boil, reduce the heat to a simmer and stir through
the onion and garlic paste. Add salt, pepper and lime juice to taste.

Serve in bowls with half the shredded chicken, topped with feta, diced avocado,
crumbled corn chips and coriander leaves. Serve with fresh lime halves and chopped
fresh chilli on the table.

MUSSELS IN CHARRED ONION & SAFFRON BROTH

SERVES 4

This Spanish-inspired sauce tastes toasty and lightly smoky from the charring of the onions. Add the snap of almonds and the delightful astringency of saffron and you've got heavenly mussels.

4 red (Spanish) onions
12 garlic cloves
400 g (14 oz) tomatoes, diced
(tinned crushed tomato is fine)
2 tablespoons paprika, lightly
toasted in a dry frying pan
(it shouldn't change colour,
just aroma)
1 small red chilli (optional)
about 100 ml (3½ fl oz)
extra virgin olive oil

12 roasted almonds, chopped
into three or four bits each
generous pinch of saffron, dry
roasted for a few seconds until
toasty but not scorched, then
soaked in 2 tablespoons water
for several hours if possible
2 kg (4 lb 8 oz) live mussels,
scrubbed and debearded

Roast the whole unpeeled onions over a flame until the outside is charred and the middle soft. You can do this in the house by scorching the outside on a stove top, then roasting in a 180°C (350°F) oven for about 25 minutes or until cooked through. Remove only the charred outside (whatever you do, don't wash the flavour off!) and pop the flesh into a food processor. Roast the garlic by constantly tossing the whole unpeeled cloves in a dry frying pan over medium–high heat until the outside skin is scorched and the middle soft: this will only take a few minutes. Squeeze the flesh into the onion mix and purée well.

Turn the oven up to 220°C (425°F). Mix the onion and garlic purée with the tomatoes, paprika, chilli (if using), olive oil, almonds and saffron in a large stockpot and simmer for 20 minutes. Season with salt and pepper (remember the mussels will add their own salt, so don't overseason at this stage) and add a touch of water if it's too thick. Spoon the mixture into a wide-based, ovenproof dish and add the mussels. Roast in the oven, stirring regularly, until the mussels open, about 10–15 minutes in total. The idea is that the sauce thickens and darkens a little, coating the open mussels, and that the mussels surrender their juices to the sauce. (You can also do this on the stove top if you want, by steaming the mussels open.)

If the mussels are alive when you cook them, they should be fine to eat even if they don't open wide, so prise open the remaining mussels. To check if uncooked mussels are alive, give open mussels a sharp tap on the bench. If it doesn't close, discard it.

Serve with crusty bread, a big bowl for the empty shells, and a glass of fine beer or unwooded white wine.

POACHED CHICKEN, SHIITAKE & SESAME SALAD

SERVES 4

I've given a recipe for how to poach a chicken (page 84), which is just fine on its own, but it's even better in this salad. Poaching your own chicken gives you a fabulous flavour, and a fabulous broth and corn to eat later. Use the shiitake stems, green ends of the onions and coriander stalks in the chicken poaching water.

meat from 1 poached chicken, shredded into bite-size bits
100 g (3½ oz) shiitake mushrooms, stalks removed, caps finely sliced
¼ Chinese cabbage (wombok), pale inside leaves only, finely shredded
handful of Thai basil leaves, torn (or use common basil)
1 bunch coriander (cilantro), leaves roughly chopped
3 spring onions (scallions), pale parts only, finely chopped
2 teaspoons sesame oil
1–2 tablespoons olive oil
2 tablespoons soy sauce
juice of 1 lime

In a big bowl toss the chicken, shiitake mushrooms, cabbage, basil, coriander and onion. Mix the combined oils with the soy sauce and lime juice, drizzle over the salad and toss to combine. Taste and add more soy in place of salt, if needed, then serve.

SWEETS

The first time I knew that a peach would change my life was when I was in France at a market in summer, and the impossibly fragrant peach I picked up refused to be handled. It was so ripe that I ended up with the skin in my hands and a face the colour of the raspberries at the stall.

The skin slips easily from a ripe peach. But it's not an experience you're likely to find often, especially if you have to buy them from shops in a country where we truck stone fruit long distances and growers could, at a pinch, be criticised for being more interested in shelf life than eating quality. When you get them close to the source, however, a simple peach is dessert perfection.

Apricots haven't yet been subverted as much and the season is still miraculously short. As anyone who has a tree can attest, however, the bought version is never the same as home-grown. Bought apricots are actually very good to cook with, which is lucky because the glut is usually big and for a month or two the prices really are on the shoppers' side.

Summer dessert might just mean stone fruit and sticky wine. Fragrant desserts and sensually wobbly jellies. A wicked pav. No-machine ice cream. It could mean cobbler or sherbet or fool. But summer dessert always means you have to leave room after dinner.

CRANACHAN
(TOASTED OATS WITH RASPBERRIES & APPLE BRANDY)

SERVES 4

It seems that the best dishes are often right under our noses. The Scottish take their beloved oats and whisky and make one of the best raspberry dishes you can imagine, using very little effort. Sometimes given the fantastic name of 'cream crowdie', Scottish cranachan may use double cream or cheese and heather honey. I use Tasmanian leatherwood honey, rolled rye, apple brandy (because I have some made locally), and single cream because it doesn't really need the richness. Take care not to overcook the rye, however, or it will taste a little too toasty.

½ cup rolled rye, or use rolled oats if you can't find rye
250 ml (9 fl oz/1 cup) pure cream (35% fat), chilled
2 tablespoons leatherwood honey
2 tablespoons apple brandy (I use Wilmot Hills), or quality whisky
150 g (5½ oz) fresh raspberries

Put the rye in a dry frying pan and gently cook over moderate heat, tossing regularly, until it becomes a lovely golden brown. Allow to cool.

Whip the cream with the honey and apple brandy until softly set. Fold in the raspberries and the oats. Refrigerate until ready to serve: within a few hours is best. You can also serve the oats on top of the cranachan to keep them crunchier, but I like the texture when they are stirred through, too.

ELDERFLOWER SHERBET WITH STRAWBERRY & BAY CREAM

SERVES 12

A sherbet, in the old fashioned sense, is an iced dessert that uses milk (unlike a sorbet) but doesn't use eggs (unlike an ice cream). This works well even if you don't have an ice-cream churn or anything too fancy. Elderflower cordial is sometimes sold as elderflower concentrate.

250 g (9 oz) sugar
250 ml (9 fl oz/1 cup) water
80 ml (2½ fl oz/⅓ cup) lemon
    juice, strained
60 ml (2 fl oz/¼ cup) elderflower
    cordial (concentrate)
400 ml (14 fl oz) full-cream milk

Strawberry and bay cream
300 ml (10½ fl oz) pure cream
    (35% fat)
1 bay leaf, fresh if possible
100 g (3½ oz) strawberries
    or raspberries
2 tablespoons icing
    (confectioners') sugar

Heat the sugar and water in a saucepan over a high heat. Stir until the sugar is dissolved. Allow to cool (speed it up by placing the pan's base in cold water), add the lemon juice and stir well. Then stir in the elderflower and milk. It could well look curdled, but don't worry about that.

Put the mixture in a largish plastic tray in the freezer (big enough to whisk it up in later) and freeze for 1 hour. Pull from the freezer and whisk (use handheld electric beaters) to break up all the ice crystals and redistribute them. Do this every half-hour or hour while the mixture freezes. If you forget it or your freezer is super-efficient and the ice becomes too firm, use a food processor to turn it back into slush or even scrape it with a fork as you would a granita. When the mixture is light and airy, freeze for another good hour so it's more like a sorbet than a slushie.

Meanwhile, make the strawberry and bay cream. In a small saucepan with a lid, heat 100 ml (3⅖ fl oz) of the cream with the bay leaf until nearly simmering. Remove from the heat, put the lid on the saucepan and allow to steep for 10 minutes. The bay leaf gives this cream a gentle spice character. Remove the lid and allow the cream to cool.

In the meantime, heat the strawberries with the tiniest bit of water to help them soften. Purée and cool this mix.

Strain the bay cream into a fresh bowl, add the remaining chilled cream and whisk until a soft moussey texture is formed. Fold in the strawberry purée and icing sugar. Serve the sherbet in glasses with a dollop of the strawberry and bay cream.

VANILLA-POACHED NECTARINES WITH CLOTTED CREAM ICE CREAM

SERVES 4

A good nectarine needs little more than to be slipped between the lips and eaten. But if you have a lot of nectarines, as happens when you grow them or buy them by the case, a good poached version makes a lovely summery dessert. Use this base recipe to poach peaches, too, swapping the wine for water and adjusting sugar to 350 g (12 oz).

220 g (7¾ oz/1 cup) sugar
700 ml (24 fl oz/2¾ cups, roughly) Sauternes-style dessert wine
1 vanilla bean, split lengthways
4 ripe nectarines

Clotted cream ice cream
2 eggs, separated
100 g (3½ oz) raw caster (superfine) sugar
1 vanilla bean
250 ml (9 fl oz/1 cup) pure cream (35% fat)
400 g (14 oz) clotted cream

To make the ice cream, beat the egg yolks with the sugar until pale and thick. Split the vanilla bean down the middle, scrape out the seeds and add this to the mixture.

In a clean bowl, whisk the eggwhites with a pinch of salt until soft peaks form. Soft peaks are the ones where they droop over as you remove the whisk. In a separate bowl, whisk the cream until it has a light, moussey texture.

Fold the clotted cream into the whipped cream then fold both into the egg yolk mixture. Fold through a quarter of the eggwhite to lighten the mix, then fold this through the remaining eggwhite, stirring just enough to get an even consistency.

Spoon into a 1 litre (35 fl oz/4 cup) shallow tray or similar, smooth off the top, and freeze for about 3 hours or until it comes away nicely with an ice-cream scoop. You don't need an ice-cream machine, but it's far better if the mixture hasn't gone really firm in the freezer when you eat it. (If it has, leave it in the fridge for 30 minutes to soften before serving.)

To poach the nectarines, put the sugar, wine and vanilla bean in a small saucepan over high heat until just simmering. Add the nectarines and poach in this liquid for about 5 minutes, or until they are soft but not soggy: it will depend a lot on the fruit. Sometimes, if really ripe, you can just bring them to the boil and turn off the heat immediately. Leave to steep in this liquid overnight, in the fridge covered with plastic wrap.

I like to peel the fruit and serve at room temperature, with the clotted cream ice cream. This is a lovely ice cream for summer fruit because the caramelly hints of the clotted cream seem to pair perfectly with the acidity of the fruit

SAFFRON PEAR & CHOCOLATE TART

SERVES 8

I've taken my favourite fruit and chocolate combination, plus my favourite chocolate tart recipe, and poshed it up with a little spice. A word of warning: the tart needs to be made well ahead so the chocolate centre can cool and set.

Pastry
150 g (5½ oz) butter, softened
150 g (5½ oz/⅔ cup) caster (superfine) sugar
3 eggs
a shade under ¼ teaspoon baking powder
300 g (10½ oz/2 cups) plain (all-purpose) flour, sifted

Ganache
125 ml (4 fl oz/½ cup) pure cream (35% fat)
2 star anise
250 g (9 oz) milk chocolate, in small pieces
2 tablespoons brandy

Poached pears
500 ml (17 fl oz/2 cups) water
200 g (7 oz) sugar
generous pinch saffron
1 tablespoon lemon juice
4 pears (preferably beurre bosc), peeled

To make the pastry, beat the butter with the sugar until pale and fluffy, add the eggs one at a time and beat until well creamed. Sift the baking powder with the flour and add to the butter mixture, stirring until just combined. Refrigerate for 1 hour.

Preheat the oven to 180°C (350°F). Roll out two-thirds of the pastry (it's easier between layers of baking paper) until it's large enough to line a 24 cm (9½ inch) pie dish. Roll the pastry over the rolling pin to pick up, and quickly lay it over the tin, lifting the sides so it slides down into the corners. Trim very roughly on the edges. Refrigerate well (or even freeze for 30 minutes) and then blind bake. To do this, line the pastry with baking paper and weigh down with uncooked beans or rice or pie weights. Bake in the oven for 10–15 minutes until starting to colour and cook through. Remove the paper and beans and bake for another 5–10 minutes at 160°C (315°F) to crisp up the base.

Roll the remaining pastry out between layers of baking paper to a diameter that will cover the tart and lay it on a baking tray in the fridge until you are ready to use it.

To make the ganache, heat the cream in a saucepan with the star anise until nearly boiling, then turn off the heat and allow to infuse for 20 minutes. Reheat the cream, strain or fish out the star anise, add the chocolate all at once and whisk until smooth. When it's all evenly textured, remove from the heat and stir in the brandy. Allow to cool.

To poach the pears, heat the water, sugar, saffron and lemon juice in a large saucepan. When simmering, add the pears (the liquid should cover them: you might need to weigh them down with a saucer so they don't float) and poach at just below a simmer until tender. Cool and store in the liquid if not using at once.

Preheat the oven to 190°C (375°F). To assemble, spread the star anise-flavoured ganache over the blind-baked pastry case. Cut the drained pears into quarters and remove the cores and stalks. Pop the pears onto the ganache. Cover the top with reserved pastry, trim to shape and press the edges to seal. Cut a small hole in the top to release air. Place the pie dish on a tray and bake for 20–25 minutes until the top is cooked. Allow to cool right down so the ganache has set and serve at room temperature, perhaps with lightly whipped cream.

GALETTE
(TO SERVE WITH APRICOTS OR PLUMS)
SERVES 8

This recipe is based on the galette Pérougienne, a fantastic dark-baked cakey thing that is delicious alone as a snack, or can be called pudding if served with a bit of fruit. Use a really good-quality cultured butter for the best results.

> 200 g (7 oz/1⅓ cups) plain (all-purpose) flour,
>   plus extra for dusting
> 7 g (¼ oz) dried yeast
> 1 teaspoon salt
> 3 tablespoons sugar
> 200 g (7 oz) cultured unsalted butter, softened
> 1 large egg
> finely grated zest of 1 lemon
> 80 ml (2½ fl oz/4 tablespoons) lukewarm water
> 2 tablespoons demerara or other raw sugar

You really don't want to knead this by hand. An electric mixer fitted with a dough hook will make your life so much easier. In the large bowl of the mixer, combine the flour and yeast with the salt and 2 tablespoons of the sugar. Add to this flour mixture 120 g (4¼ oz) of the butter with the egg, lemon zest and warm water, and knead until you have a soft dough.

Shape the dough into what could be a rough ball (it can be a bit sticky and soft), and pop it in a large greased bowl. Cover with a damp cloth or plastic wrap and set it aside to rise in a warm spot until just doubled in size, about an hour, maybe two.

Preheat the oven to 230°C (450°F) or whatever its maximum is, up to 250°C (500°F). Line a baking tray with baking paper. Press the dough into a 25 cm (10 inch) round about 1 cm (⅜ inch) thick, leaving a slightly raised border at the edge. Sprinkle the remaining sugar and all the demerara sugar over the dough (avoiding this rim) and dot with the remaining butter.

Transfer to the prepared baking tray and bake in the centre of the oven for 12–15 minutes until dark in places and caramelised. Darker is better than lighter for this. Take it out of the oven and leave to cool on the tray for 5 minutes at least, then serve warm or cool, with some fruit so you don't feel like you're just eating sugar, butter and flour.

DRUNKEN RASPBERRIES
WITH CLOTTED CREAM
SERVES 4

Most of the raspberries we grow on the farm—at least while the garden is being established—are eaten standing next to the raspberry canes. But the glut in early January is so large that a lot do make it into the house and we occasionally jazz them up with other things. Here, it's just good old vodka from our friend Bill McHenry (of William McHenry and Sons Distillery) and some delicious clotted cream.

300 g (10½ oz) fresh raspberries
2 tablespoons vodka
1 tablespoon icing (confectioners') sugar, sifted
about 100 g (3½ oz) clotted cream, or similar

Mix the raspberries with the vodka and sugar and allow to stand for 20 minutes. Serve the fruit with the clotted cream, or try the golden syrup ice cream on page 192.

SADIE'S APRICOT COBBLER
SERVES 4

My cobbler (well, actually the cobbler perfected by my partner, Sadie) isn't made by putting scone dough on top of fruit, like some. It's more a batter that you slip fruit into. And it's seriously good. You can use most fruits, even cooked quinces, but apricots are of the moment, especially if you have a tree, so every opportunity to use up the glut is welcome. If your apricots are really sour, use 75 g (2¾ oz) of sugar for the top.

50 g (1¾ oz) butter
100 g (3½ oz/⅔ cup) plain (all-purpose) flour
100 g (3½ oz/scant ½ cup) caster (superfine) sugar
2 teaspoons baking powder
pinch of salt
170 ml (5½ fl oz/⅔ cup) milk
about 450 g (1 lb) apricots or other fruit, halved, stones removed

Preheat the oven to 200°C (400°F). In a 2 litre (70 fl oz/8 cup) casserole dish or similar melt the butter in the oven while you make the batter.

With a wooden spoon mix the flour, half of the sugar, the baking powder and salt. Stir in the milk and beat just until you have a nice even batter. Pour this batter onto the melted butter. DO NOT STIR. Lay the halved fruit on top and sprinkle the remaining sugar on top. Pop the dish into the centre of the oven, turn the temperature down to 180°C (350°F) and bake for 1 hour.

The edges should start to caramelise and the fruit will sink into the swelling batter. Serve hot with golden syrup ice cream (page 192) or a little drizzle of cream.

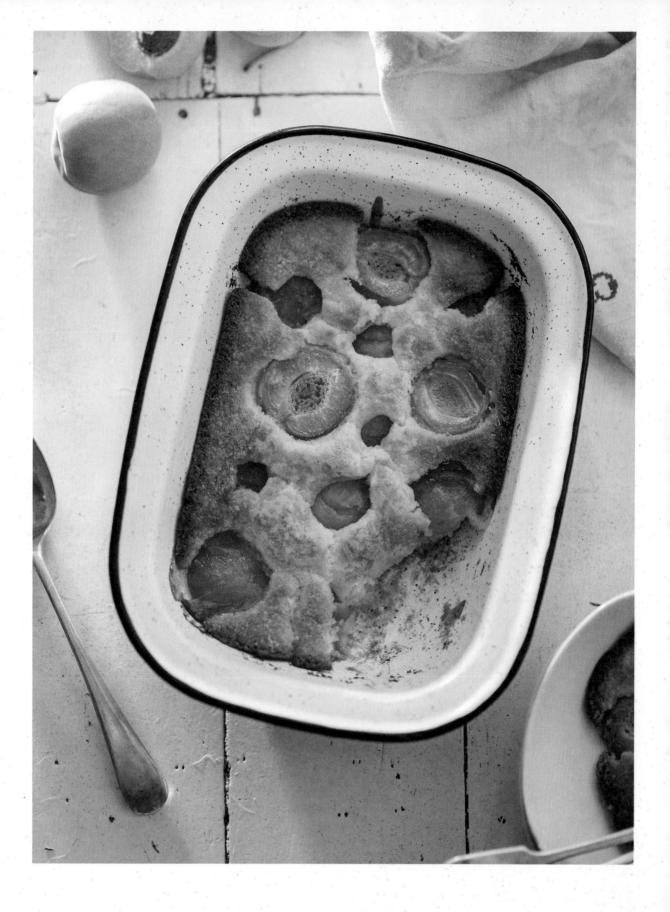

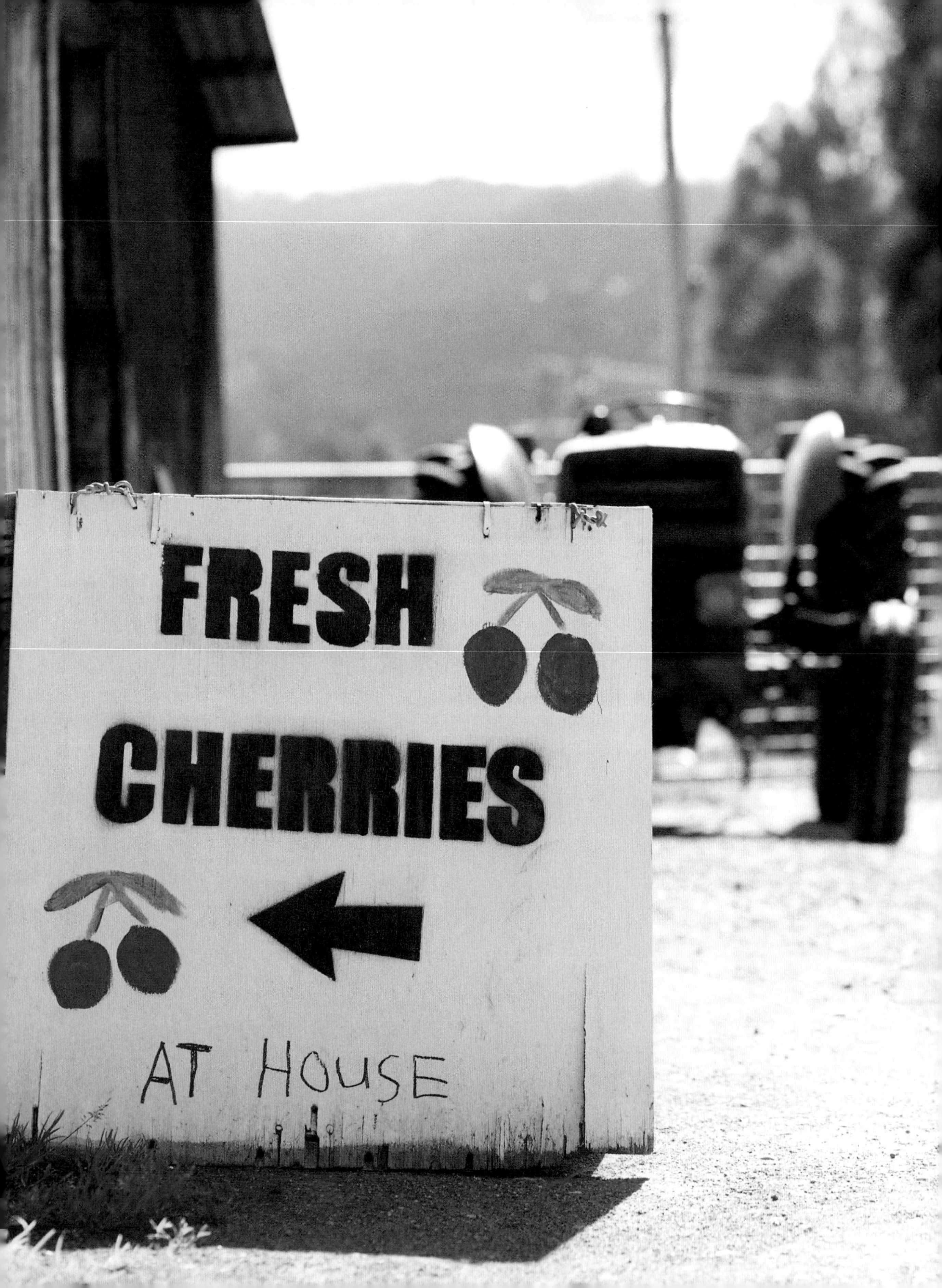
FRESH
CHERRIES
AT HOUSE

WHITE PEACHES WITH BLUEBERRIES & SAUVIGNON BLANC JELLY

SERVES 4

It's nice to serve summer fruit in a soft, giving jelly. It's even nicer if
that jelly is made with a lively wine. Depending on your wine, the sugar
quantity might vary. To poach the peaches, you could use the recipe for
vanilla-poached nectarines (page 156), and use the poaching liquid
(without adding more sugar) to make this jelly.

300 ml (10½ fl oz) sauvignon blanc
200 ml (7 fl oz) water
about 60 g (2¼ oz) sugar
2 teaspoons powdered gelatine
2 poached white peaches, peeled, stones removed, cut into wedges
60 ml (2 fl oz/¼ cup) pure cream (35% fat), lightly whipped
    (or use a nice-quality yoghurt), for serving
about 50 g (1¾ oz) blueberries, for serving

Heat the wine in a saucepan with the water and sugar and stir until dissolved. Bring
close to the boil (simmer if you want to dissipate the alcohol) and sprinkle in the
gelatine, stirring rapidly to dissolve. Cool the jelly well, but not so much that it sets.

Distribute the peach pieces evenly into the bottom of four glass dishes that you
will serve it in, and pour the jelly over them.

Allow to set overnight in the fridge and serve with the cream and blueberries.

RASPBERRY & ELDERFLOWER TRIFLE WITH MOSCATO JELLY

SERVES 8 AT LEAST

Elderflowers have a tremendous summery perfume and the cordial (concentrate) is widely available at supermarkets. Failing that, just use freshly squeezed orange juice. If you can't get moscato, dilute a dessert wine with half its volume in water.

600 ml (21 fl oz) moscato wine
2 teaspoons powdered gelatine
8 savoiardi (lady fingers) biscuits
at least 300 g (10½ oz) fresh raspberries
4 eggs, separated
50 g (1¾ oz) caster (superfine) sugar
130 g (4½ oz/1 cup) icing (confectioners') sugar
500 g (1 lb 2 oz) mascarpone
4 tablespoons (about ⅓ cup) elderflower cordial (concentrate)

Start the day before you want to eat it.

Heat the moscato until it nearly boils. Whisk in the gelatine so it dissolves. Arrange the savoiardi in the base of a 25 cm (10 inch) square casserole dish or similar and tip the moscato mixture over them. Cool, then pop into the fridge so it sets. Best to give it overnight. The next day tip half the raspberries over the top.

Whisk the eggwhites with the sugar until light yet stiff. Whisk the egg yolks with the icing sugar until pale and fluffy, then beat in the mascarpone but don't overbeat because it can split. Stir in the cordial and then gently fold in the eggwhite mixture. Smear this thickly over the jelly and raspberries, top with more raspberries, cover and put back in the fridge to set for an hour or two. Serve with more moscato as a drink.

BASIL-SCENTED CARAMELISED STRAWBERRIES
SERVES 2

Take an average strawberry, add warmth, and it'll lift the flavour, almost unbelievably so. Take a great strawberry and the results will make you swoon. I also occasionally use rose geranium for this, rather than basil, which gives a different but equally interesting result.

2 tablespoons sugar
250 g (9 oz) strawberries, stems removed, halved
a good splash of white, rosé or red wine (whatever
   you've got in the house)
2 fresh basil leaves, finely shredded (or toss in
   1 whole rose geranium leaf)

Heat the sugar in a frying pan, shaking regularly until it starts to caramelise. It should be golden, not black. Toss in the strawberries, allow to cook a little, then splash in the wine (about ¼ cup), add the basil or rose geranium and toss to melt the caramel and boil off the alcohol. Serve immediately with cream or lemon leaf custard (page 179) or golden syrup ice cream (page 192).

YOGHURT & RASPBERRY CAKE
WITH ELDERFLOWER SYRUP

SERVES 8–10

This is a variation on a Greek-inspired yoghurt cake I've been making for some years. The raspberries tend to sink into the batter a bit as the cake rises, which is just perfect.

125 g (4½ oz) butter, softened
200 g (7 oz) caster (superfine) sugar
3 eggs
finely grated zest and strained juice of ½ lemon
 (1 tablespoon juice and ½ teaspoon zest)
200 g (7 oz/1½ cups) self-raising flour
200 g (7 oz/¾ cup) natural yoghurt
150 g (5½ oz) raspberries
80 ml (2½ fl oz/⅓ cup) water
150 g (5½ oz) sugar
1 tablespoon elderflower cordial (concentrate)

Preheat the oven to 180°C (350°F). Grease a 20 cm (8 inch) round cake tin and line the base and side with baking paper.

Beat the butter and sugar together until pale and fluffy. Beat in the eggs, one at a time. It may look a bit curdled but don't worry, we'll fix that. Gently fold in the lemon zest and flour and then fold in the yoghurt too. Use a spatula to scrape into the cake tin, making the centre a little lower compared to the edges. Dot the raspberries over the top. Bake for 30–40 minutes until a skewer comes out clean.

While the cake cooks, heat the water, sugar and lemon juice in a small saucepan and simmer for 5 minutes. When the cake is cooked, take it from the oven, but leave it in the tin. Poke a fine skewer into the cake about 30 times all over. Remove the syrup from the heat and add the elderflower cordial, then spoon the syrup over the top of the cake. Try to spoon it so it soaks into the holes evenly rather than all soaking into the edges around the tin. Allow to cool, then serve on a picnic rug, in dappled shade, in summer, or spring, or winter, or autumn.

Cold winters mean lush summer fruit, with an intensity and bracing acidity that makes you go weak at the knees.

We cook summer fruit. When we must.

HRISTINA'S CHERRY STRUDEL
SERVES 4

This stunningly easy recipe comes from a wonderful cook and friend
Hristina, who lives in Hobart and who harvests and pits her own cherries
from the Huon Valley every summer. If you're using frozen cherries, only
let them half defrost before using or they will leach too much juice into
the pastry. I used a packet of filo pastry and made three strudels to serve
about four people from each one.

> 125 g (4½ oz/6 sheets) filo pastry
> grapeseed oil, for drizzling
> about 100 g (3½ oz) caster (superfine) sugar
> 150 g (5½ oz) fresh or frozen pitted cherries; use sour cherries
>   such as kentish or morellos if you can
> 1 tablespoon semolina
> icing (confectioners') sugar, for dusting

Preheat the oven to 180°C (350°F). Line a baking sheet with baking paper.

Work really fast with the filo pastry. Lay out a sheet with the short edge towards
you and use a spoon held vertically in the oil then twizzled about to just dribble and
spot a bit of oil, not a whole lot. Sprinkle evenly but quickly with about 2–3 teaspoons
of caster sugar. Lay the next sheet on top, offset by 2–3 cm (about an inch) to the right
of the first so it overhangs at the edge. Oil and sugar as before. Lay the next sheet
2–3 cm to the left of the original and oil and sugar too. The overhanging edges will
fold in to hold the cherries in the strudel. Lay the next three sheets of filo on top of
the original sheet, one by one, oiling and sugaring as you go. Scatter the cherries over
one-third of the pastry closest to you, leaving the overhanging edges without cherries.
Sprinkle the cherries with the semolina and roll, starting with the base closest to
you and folding in the overhanging edges at the same time so the cherries don't
escape. Roll tightly until the strudel is completely rolled up, with the loose edge right
underneath. Brush the top with a tiny bit of oil and transfer to the prepared baking
sheet. Bake in the oven for 20–30 minutes until well browned. The trick Hristina
taught me was to press the pastry and feel it crisp in layers, not soft and squashy
under the surface: that way you know it's done.

Cool well, slice, then dust liberally with icing sugar and serve. The strudel
is crisp the same day; the next day the pastry will soften, but be just as good.

APPLE & MULBERRY PIE WITH LATTICE TOP & LEMON LEAF CUSTARD

SERVES 8

We get two flushes of mulberries in the Huon Valley. One is early in summer, the other nearly autumn, when the first of the apples are ripening. While mulberries are best just gobbled up, if you have a few, a handful in a pie is a pretty nice treat. For the apple we use gravensteins as that's what is ripe early, but at other times a firm cooking variety such as golden delicious or granny smith works well; any sharp variety is usually good.

100 g (3½ oz) caster (superfine) sugar
750 g (1 lb 10 oz) apples
150 g mulberries, or use blackberries or other dark berries out of season
1 tablespoon cornflour (cornstarch)
about 50 g (1¾ oz) butter, chilled and cut into small dice
lemon leaf custard (see opposite), for serving

Pastry
200 g (7 oz/1⅓ cups) plain (all-purpose) flour
120 g (4¼ oz) butter (or, even better, an equal combination
    of butter and lard, chilled and diced)
1 egg yolk
about 2 tablespoons iced water

To make the pastry, blend the flour and butter in a food processor, until just combined and the mixture looks like breadcrumbs. Pulse in the egg yolk and just enough iced water to combine. Tip the mixture onto a clean bench and press together to make a ball. Wrap tightly in plastic wrap and pop into the fridge to rest for 30 minutes.

Roll out two-thirds of the pastry and line a 22 cm (8½ inch) diameter pie dish or similar. Sprinkle the pie base with half the sugar. Peel, core and cut the apples into 12 wedges each. Toss the mulberries, remaining sugar and cornflour together in a bowl, then gently stir through the apple to just evenly mix. Press this fruit into the lined pie dish and scatter the butter over the top.

Now, it gets a bit tricky to explain, but you're trying to weave pastry strips for the top, so let's give it a crack. Roll out the remaining pastry to a 4 mm (⅙ inch) thick, 23 cm (9 inch) round and cut it into 10 strips. To make the lattice, lay 5 strips horizontally across the pie, using ones that are the right length, about 2 cm (¾ inch) apart, then fold every second pastry strip back on itself to halfway.

Lay a fresh strip of pastry perpendicular to the horizontal strips just off the centre, then unfold every second horizontal strip and lay them back down. Fold back the pastry strips that weren't folded back last time until they reach the vertical strip.

Lay a second fresh strip of pastry perpendicular to the horizontal strips and lay the horizontal strips back down. Repeat until you use up the remaining strips. Sounds complicated but it isn't. If you're really stuck, find a video of it online.

Bake for 40 minutes or until the pastry is golden and the apples are tender. Serve with the custard.

▼▼▼▼▼▼▼▼▼▼▼▼▼▼▼▼▼▼▼▼▼▼▼▼▼▼▼▼▼▼▼▼

LEMON LEAF CUSTARD
MAKES 1 LITRE (35 FL OZ/4 CUPS)

> 1 litre (35 fl oz/4 cups) milk
> 3–4 fresh lemon leaves, well washed
> 2 tablespoons cornflour (cornstarch)
> 6 eggs
> 100 g (3½ oz) sugar

Heat the milk with the lemon leaves in a medium saucepan over high heat until nearly boiling. Turn off the heat and allow to steep for 15 minutes. Use a little of this milk to mix with the cornflour in a bowl, then whisk in the eggs and sugar. Reheat the remaining milk, strain and whisk into the egg mixture. Pour this back into a clean saucepan, return to high heat and continue whisking or stirring until the custard thickens and comes to the boil. Remove from the heat immediately and cover the surface of the custard with plastic wrap, or whisk often, to prevent a skin forming.

LEMON BRÛLÉE TART

SERVES 8–10

This sprightly, bright golden tart (if you use superb eggs!) has a lovely lemon tang. It looks a bit neater to glaze slices after it's cut, but I quite like presenting the whole tart and cracking through the caramel to get through to the creamy base.

6 eggs
300 g (10½ oz/1⅓ cups) caster
  (superfine) sugar
juice of 5 lemons, not strained
250 ml (9 fl oz/1 cup) thick
  (double/heavy) cream
finely grated zest of 3 lemons
icing (confectioners') sugar,
  for dusting

Shortcrust

180 g (6¼ oz) butter, softened
finely grated zest of 2 lemons
120 g (4¼ oz) icing
  (confectioners') sugar
300 g (10½ oz/2 cups) plain
  (all-purpose) flour
about 1–2 tablespoons iced water

To make the shortcrust, grease and line a 24 cm (9½ inch) flan (tart) tin with a removable base or similar. Mix the butter with the lemon zest and icing sugar until well combined. Add the flour and mix just until it comes together. Add enough iced water and knead just enough to make a smooth dough. Refrigerate for 1 hour.

Preheat the oven to 180°C (350°F). Roll out the pastry (it's easier between layers of baking paper) until it's large enough to line the tin. Roll the pastry over the rolling pin to pick up, and quickly lay it over the tin, lifting the sides so it slides down into the corners. Trim very roughly on the edges. Refrigerate well (or even freeze for 30 minutes) and then blind bake. To do this, line the shortcrust with baking paper and weigh down with uncooked beans or rice or pie weights. Bake for 10–15 minutes until starting to colour and cook through. Remove the paper and beans and bake for another 5–10 minutes at about 160°C (315°F) to crisp up the base.

Remove the shortcrust from the oven and turn the oven down to 120°C (250°F).

To make the filling, whisk the eggs with the sugar and lemon juice until well combined. Whisk in the cream and allow the mixture to sit for at least an hour before gently removing the froth with a spoon. Pour through a sieve, remove any froth or bubbles on top, then add the lemon zest. Pour this mixture into the hot tart case (if you're pedantic, you can pop any remaining bubbles with a toothpick) and bake for 25–35 minutes until just set. The way to check if it's set is to give it a gentle bump and watch if it wobbles in the centre. When it's not wobbling, remove it from the oven and cool completely before removing from the tin. Dust the top with icing sugar and use a blowtorch (if you have one) to caramelise the top lightly. If not, just use a nice dusting of icing sugar. Cool completely before serving. It shouldn't need cream.

GOOSEBERRY & ELDERFLOWER FOOL
SERVES 4–6

I kind of hope that if more kids are exposed to the kitchen we'll be eating better in a few years' time. Here's a recipe they can make or help with the mixing over the summer holidays. And if they don't get into cooking, at least they can laugh at the name. A fool is something stirred through custard or cream. Here I've used both. You can use the same philosophy to make other summer fools, such as raspberry or strawberry.

1 kg (2 lb 4 oz) gooseberries
100 g (3½ oz) sugar
2 tablespoons elderflower cordial (concentrate)
500 ml (17 fl oz/2 cups) thick, Home-made Lemon Custard (see below), chilled and pushed through a sieve
500 ml (17 fl oz/2 cups) pure cream (35% fat), whipped until thick

Remove any stalks from the gooseberries and wash well. Drain, put them in a pan with the sugar and stew until really soft. Push vigorously through a sieve and discard the skins. Cool, add the elderflower cordial, and then fold very gently through the combined custard and whipped cream, adding more sugar to taste.

▼▼▼▼▼▼▼▼▼▼▼▼▼▼▼▼▼▼▼▼▼▼▼▼▼▼▼▼▼▼▼

PROPER THICK HOME-MADE LEMON CUSTARD
MAKES ABOUT 750 G (1 LB 10 OZ)

600 ml (21 fl oz) milk
4 strips lemon rind, taken with a potato peeler
4 tablespoons cornflour (cornstarch)
3 eggs, lightly beaten
100 g (3½ oz) sugar
1 teaspoon natural vanilla essence

Heat the milk with the lemon rind in a small saucepan over high heat until it starts to foam. Turn off the heat and allow to stand for 10 minutes. Reheat the milk until nearly boiling. While it heats, mix the cornflour with just enough milk to dissolve it, in a large bowl. (If you want a thinner custard, reduce the cornflour by half.) Add the eggs and sugar and whisk well. Whisk the hot milk into this mixture and then strain into a clean saucepan. Return to the stove over high heat and, whisking constantly, bring back to the boil. Remove from the heat, cover with plastic wrap and allow to cool.

LEMON CURD
MAKES ABOUT 1 KG (2 LB 4 OZ)

I probably don't need to give you a recipe for lemon curd. You probably already have one. But it's just soooo good with the pavlova (page 189), plus you can use it on your toast, with the saffron doughnuts (page 203) or in a tart: I simply can't resist.

        finely grated zest and strained juice of 6 lemons
        8 eggs, lightly beaten
        200 g (7 oz) unsalted butter
        400 g (14 oz) caster (superfine) sugar

In the top of a double-boiler, or in a heatproof bowl set over a small saucepan of simmering water, melt all the ingredients together, stirring occasionally with a wooden spoon. Once melted, keep stirring over boiling water until thickened slightly, scraping the bottom as you stir. This will take about 10 minutes, but could be as little as 5 or as long as 15 minutes.

      The mixture will thicken, and don't worry if there are a couple of lumps—they prove it's homemade. It also thickens more as it cools. Transfer to sterile jars and store in the fridge for up to a month. Serve on sourdough toast, in tarts or with sharp fruits such as rhubarb or raspberries. Oh, and with pavlova.

STRAWBERRY & ROSE PETAL SHORTCAKE

SERVES ABOUT 10

Yes, strawberries again. Not that they always need cooking. Strawberries should be ripe and fab right now with barely more than a splash of elderflower cordial or a sprinkle of sugar and some runny cream. But you can cook them into the most memorable dishes, like this one, with the fragrance of exquisite rose petals. Okay, if you really insist.

200 g (7 oz) butter, softened
200 g (7 oz) caster (superfine) sugar
4 eggs
½ teaspoon natural vanilla essence
400 g (14 oz) plain (all-purpose) flour
nearly ¼ teaspoon baking powder
50 g (1¾ oz) caster (superfine) sugar, extra
500 g (1 lb 2 oz) strawberries, stems removed, halved
a handful of unsprayed fragrant rose petals, washed and patted dry
finely grated zest of 1 lemon
more caster sugar, for sprinkling

Beat the butter and caster sugar together until pale and fluffy, then beat in the eggs one at a time. Beat in the vanilla essence. Sift the flour together with the baking powder and fold in gently. Cover and refrigerate for 1 hour.

Preheat the oven to 190°C (375°F). Grease a 24 cm (9½ inch) diameter pie dish and sprinkle it with sugar (this makes it a bit nonstick). Roll two-thirds of the shortcake mix out between layers of baking paper and use it to line the pie dish. Roll out the other third, cover and return to the fridge until ready to assemble.

Mix the extra caster sugar with the strawberries, rose petals and lemon zest and fill the pie case. Top with the reserved rolled-out dough. Press the edges to seal, cut a slit into the top, and sprinkle the top with a fine dusting of more caster sugar. Bake in the middle of the oven for 30–40 minutes. Test with a skewer as you would a cake. Allow to cool before serving with lightly whipped cream or vanilla ice cream, or even a lovely balsamic ice cream.

APPLE & SAFFRON TEACAKE

MAKES 1 LARGE CAKE

Light and bright, this cake is like the summer sun on a plate. It's best to soak the saffron overnight, to extract as much flavour as you can. In a pinch you can do it for a few hours, or even heat some of the milk with the saffron to speed up the process. If it's too soon for apples, use new-season pears, as they usually ripen earlier.

generous pinch of saffron
185 ml (6 fl oz/¾ cup) milk
75 g (2¾ oz) butter, softened
225 g (8 oz) caster (superfine) sugar
3 eggs
300 g (10½ oz/2 cups) self-raising flour
1 teaspoon natural vanilla essence
2 medium apples, preferably a cooking variety,
    peeled, cored and cut into wedges
60 g (2¼ oz/¼ cup firmly packed) brown sugar
½ teaspoon ground cinnamon

Soak the saffron in 1–2 tablespoons of the milk, overnight if possible.

Preheat the oven to 170°C (325°F). Grease and line a 22 cm (8¾ inch) springform cake tin. Beat the butter and caster sugar together until pale and fluffy, then beat in the eggs one at a time.

Fold in the flour, remaining milk, vanilla and saffron milk mixture, and stir until just combined and evenly textured. Pour this cake batter into the greased tin and dot evenly with the apple wedges.

Mix the brown sugar and cinnamon and sprinkle over the top of the cake. Bake in the centre of the oven for 30–40 minutes until a skewer inserted in the middle of the cake comes out clean.

Allow to cool in the tin for 10 minutes, then remove the tin, cool completely and serve, perhaps with runny cream.

PEACH & RASPBERRY PAVLOVA THAT'S SPECIAL ENOUGH FOR CHRISTMAS

SERVES 10

If you have a warm Christmas, as we do, you can leave the heavy pudding for some other time. Bring on the pav—always in fashion, always delicious— here made using the best of the summer fruit. If you can't find good, fragrant, fully ripe nectarines, you can use peaches, or simply load it up with a mix of berries. And if it's not Christmas, make it just because.

6 eggs, separated
360 g (12¾ oz) caster (superfine)
    sugar
1 teaspoon white wine vinegar
2 teaspoons cornflour (cornstarch)
a few drops of natural vanilla
    essence
375 g (13 oz) mascarpone
200 ml (7 fl oz) pure cream
    (35% fat), lightly whipped
2–3 drops rosewater (optional)
3 tablespoons icing
    (confectioners') sugar

1 vanilla bean
300 g (10½ oz) raspberries
100 g (3½ oz) blackcurrants
50 g (1¾ oz) sugar
1 tablespoon water
250 ml (9 fl oz/1 cup) lemon curd
    (page 184)
2 peaches
100 g (3½ oz) blueberries or
    silvanberries, or both

Preheat the oven to 160°C (315°F). Beat the eggwhites until soft peaks form, then whisk in the sugar, then the vinegar, cornflour and vanilla essence. The mixture should be stiff by now. Tip onto a baking tray lined with baking paper and use a spatula to form a steep-sided round, 6 cm (2⅜ inch) high and 25 cm (10 inches) diameter.

Bake for 10 minutes, then reduce the oven to 140°C (275°F) and bake for about 90 minutes, checking that it doesn't brown too much—if at all—and turning down the oven further as need be. Allow to cool in the turned-off oven (some modern ovens may need to be wedged open so the meringue doesn't sweat).

Combine the mascarpone, cream, rosewater (if using), icing sugar and seeds scraped from the vanilla bean. Stir well, taking care not to overwhip or the mixture will split. Heat half the raspberries over gentle heat to break them down to a sauce. Allow to cool and stir, in one or two quick motions, into the mascarpone mixture so it's kind of rippled.

Heat the blackcurrants with the sugar and water in a small saucepan over high heat to melt and soften. When fruit is soft, press through a sieve and discard solids.

Spread lemon curd over the top of the pav, cover with the mascarpone mixture, then garnish with sliced peaches, the remaining raspberries and the blueberries and silvanberries if you have them. Drizzle on the blackcurrant syrup to serve.

HONEY & VANILLA BEAN
MILK JELLY

SERVES 4

Some might call this a latte cotto, a lighter, less rich variation on pannacotta. I wouldn't dare do that. Instead, I'll just say it's a lovely way to finish a meal when the weather's stinking hot and you just want a gentle end to the perfect day.

650 ml (22½ fl oz) full-cream (full-fat) milk
2 tablespoons honey
80 g (2¾ oz) sugar
1 vanilla bean, split lengthways and seeds scraped
50 ml (1¾ fl oz) water
15 g (½ oz) powdered gelatine
250 g (9 oz) fresh blueberries and raspberries

Heat the milk, honey, sugar and vanilla bean seeds with the vanilla pod in a saucepan over medium heat, stirring until the sugar is dissolved. Remove from the heat, scoop out the vanilla pod (you can wash and dry it and use for vanilla sugar or custard and so on) and set aside the milk for a minute.

Put the water in a heatproof bowl and set it over a small saucepan of simmering water. Sprinkle the gelatine in and stir until it dissolves.

Whisk this gelatine mixture into the milk mixture, then pour into a 750 ml (26 fl oz/3 cup) jelly mould or similar. Allow to cool well before covering with plastic wrap and refrigerating overnight.

When you're ready to serve, turn the jelly out of its mould (perhaps by running hot water over the mould to loosen it) and tip it onto a serving platter. Scatter berries around the jelly and serve.

HONEY, PISTACHIO & SAFFRON KULFI

SERVES 4–6

Kulfi is a lovely spiced Indian frozen dessert made from reduced milk.
The trick is to boil the milk down fast enough that you don't get bored,
without boiling it over. You can, if you're into really sweet things, use
sweetened condensed milk and omit the sugar, but the real thing from
scratch is so much nicer.

1.5 litres (52 fl oz/6 cups) milk
2 teaspoons cornflour (cornstarch)
generous pinch of saffron
8 green cardamom pods
50 g (1¾ oz) sugar, or adjust to taste
10 g (⅜ oz/about 1 tablespoon) sliced pistachios
2 tablespoons honey
more pistachios and honey, for serving

Mix 100 ml (3½ fl oz) of the milk with the cornflour and whisk until there are no
lumps. Sprinkle in the saffron and set aside.

Boil the remaining milk with the cardamom pods in a very large frying pan or
wide-based shallow saucepan over medium–high heat. The wider the base and lower
the sides of the pan, the quicker it will evaporate. Occasionally stir the bottom and
sides of the frying pan to prevent the milk scalding.

After the milk comes to the boil, stir just enough to stop it boiling over or
scalding, until it is reduced to half its volume. You can check this by pouring it into
a heatproof jug to measure if it is down to 700 ml (24 fl oz). Strain or fish out the
cardamom pods and discard them, then whisk the milk into the cornflour mixture and
return it to the stove in a clean saucepan. Turn up the heat, stirring constantly, until
the mixture comes to the boil. Then turn right down, stir in the sugar, pistachios and
honey, and cook for a further 2 minutes.

Turn off the heat, cover with a layer of plastic wrap with a few holes spiked into
it and allow to cool to room temperature, then pour into an 800 ml (28 fl oz) mould
or four individual moulds. Cover the surface of the kulfi with plastic wrap. Put it in
the freezer for 6 hours or overnight. When nearly ready to serve, transfer it from the
freezer to the fridge for half an hour. Dip the mould in hot water and tip the kulfi out
onto a plate. Serve with more crushed pistachios and some extra honey drizzled over.

NO-MACHINE GOLDEN SYRUP ICE CREAM

SERVES 8–10

This is a lightly flavoured ice cream designed to go with or without something else sweet. If you want a more robust golden syrup flavour, increase the golden syrup to 200 g (7 oz) and cut the glucose syrup to 75 g (2¾ oz). But for my money, this is just about perfect as is.

6 eggs, separated
150 g (5½ oz) golden syrup (light treacle)
300 ml (10½ fl oz) pure cream (35% fat)
300 ml (10½ fl oz) sour cream (don't use low-fat sour cream)
100 g (3½ oz) glucose syrup (corn syrup)
pinch of salt

Whisk the egg yolks with the golden syrup until pale and fluffy. Stir this into the combined cream and sour cream, then continue whisking until it is the texture of very lightly whipped cream.

Whisk the eggwhites with the glucose and salt until soft peaks form. Gently fold a quarter of the eggwhite mixture into the cream mixture until nearly combined, then fold this lightened mixture into the remaining eggwhite mixture until it has an even consistency. Scoop and scrape into an ice cream container and freeze for at least 3–4 hours or until frozen.

It keeps well for a few days, but it's best consumed in about a week.

WARM STRAWBERRY & SAFFRON SALAD WITH VANILLA DRAINED YOGHURT
SERVES 4

We get a steady stream of strawberries growing all summer, and whoever is in the garden usually gets the lion's share. It's worth taking some back to the farmhouse, however, to make this stunning dessert. I've left the yoghurt quite sharp, despite its vanilla content, to counter and lift the flavour of the fruit, but you can lace it with a little icing sugar if you have a sweeter tooth.

> 500 g (1 lb 2 oz) Greek-style yoghurt
> pinch of saffron threads
> 2 teaspoons natural vanilla essence
> 2 tablespoons honey
> 1 tablespoon finely sliced or grated lemon zest
> 500 g (1 lb 2 oz) fragrant, ripe strawberries, stems removed
> 3 peaches or nectarines, stoned, cut into chunks
> 1 tablespoon lemon juice
> 5 basil leaves, finely sliced

Put the yoghurt in a strainer lined with muslin (cheesecloth) or strong, clean, absorbent paper towel. Cover the yoghurt, place a bowl underneath the strainer, and pop the lot in the fridge to let the whey drain out overnight. Pop the saffron into a tiny amount of water, about 2 teaspoons, and allow to steep overnight as well.

The next day, put the thickish yoghurt into a bowl (discard the whey) and stir in the vanilla.

In a large frying pan, heat the honey with the lemon zest and saffron with its soaking water. Add the fruit and toss to just warm through. Add the lemon juice and basil, toss again, and serve with the yoghurt.

NOT ETON MESS

SERVES 5–6

Okay, so you don't need to use a recipe to eat raspberries, you just need fingers. But if they're soft and lush and you want a seriously scrummy dessert in minutes, fold them into my version of England's Eton mess. Traditionally made with banana or strawberries, Eton mess is a jumble of meringue with cream and fruit, and I find the acidity of raspberries also works really well. Recipes often omit the ice cream in favour of more whipped cream, but this one suits our climate better.

> 250 ml (9 fl oz/1 cup) pure cream (35% fat), chilled
> ½ teaspoon orange blossom water
> 2 tablespoons caster (superfine) sugar
> 250 ml (9 fl oz/1 cup) quality vanilla ice cream,
>   softened ever so slightly
> handful of crumbled meringue
> 150 g (5½ oz) raspberries, or more to taste or budget

Whip the cream with the orange blossom water and sugar until soft and moussey. Fold in spoonfuls of the ice cream, meringue and raspberries. Serve immediately.

RASPBERRY & WHITE CHOCOLATE TIPSY CAKE

SERVES 6

This dessert relies on good-quality ricotta; the stuff you get from a deli, not a supermarket cabinet in a tub. You make it as you would a tiramisu, even if the flavours are nothing like those of a tiramisu. A glass serving dish or similar would work well.

500 g (1 lb 2 oz) fresh ricotta cheese (see page 37)
150 g (5½ oz) icing (confectioners') sugar
2 tablespoons finely grated orange zest
2 teaspoons natural vanilla essence
100 ml (3½ fl oz) pure cream (35% fat)
100 g (3½ oz) raspberries
50 g (1¾ oz) white chocolate, grated, plus extra for decorating
250 ml (9 fl oz/1 cup) strong Earl Grey tea, cooled
125 ml (4 fl oz/½ cup) Marsala or similar fortified wine
250 g (9 oz) savoiardi (lady fingers) biscuits

In the bowl of an electric mixer, beat the ricotta with the sugar, orange zest and vanilla until well combined. Slowly add the cream and continue to beat for 30 seconds until light and creamy. Fold in the raspberries and chocolate.

To assemble the trifle, first get out the 2 litre (70 fl oz/8 cup) dish you will set it in: glass works well, though a nice ceramic dish also looks the goods. Mix the tea with the Marsala in a medium bowl and start to soak the savoiardi until they're just wet through. It takes a few seconds for them to absorb the liquid, but just do a few at a time and use them before adding more to the liquid. When they're moistened, line the bowl or dish with half of the biscuits, scoop half of the ricotta mixture over, then top with the remaining soaked biscuits. Cover with the remaining ricotta mixture, spreading it evenly over the top. Sprinkle with grated chocolate and leave in the fridge for a couple of hours, at least, to set.

Serve with glasses of a sweet moscato wine or wee cups of espresso coffee.

Summer means raspberries as dark and deeply red as a bruised thumb; it means cherry spitting and mulberry gathering.

BAKED BITS

We do like a few bits and pieces from the oven, even in the warmer months. A honey bun to have with our own devilishly smoky bacon? Yes, please. A few spiced biscuits to share over drinks? You bet. A little saffron doughnut, perhaps (even though it's fried, not baked)? Or a flatbread, or Sadie's glorious whisky walnut bickies to have with a little coffee after dinner? Yes, yes, yes.

Baking a few grissini won't roast the house for long. Flatbreads can be made out of the oven. And what would a southern hemisphere festive season be without a little mince tart to leave out for Santa when he comes bashing through the bush on his wallaby-drawn sleigh? Don't forget the whisky to go with it, thank you very much.

SAFFRON & CURRANT DOUGHNUTS IN CARDAMOM SUGAR

MAKES 8 DOUGHNUTS

My neighbour in Tasmania grows saffron, so I've learnt two important things: don't grow it yourself if your neighbour does (it's really hard work and you need to have good knees and back to pick it); and it's best to soak the saffron overnight to extract the flavour. I've cooked these doughnuts in pork fat because they taste terrific that way and we're lucky enough to have plenty of lard kicking round the house, but vegetable oil is just fine.

good pinch of saffron
200 ml (7 fl oz) tepid water
  (body temperature)
7 g (¼ oz/1 sachet) dried yeast
1 teaspoon sugar
290 g (10¼ oz) plain (all-purpose)
  flour
½ teaspoon salt
roughly 50 g (1¾ oz) lard or butter

150 g (5½ oz) currants,
  soaked in 1 tablespoon rum
  for an hour or two
100 g (3½ oz) caster (superfine)
  sugar
1 tablespoon ground cardamom
500 g (1 lb 2 oz) pork fat,
  for deep-frying (or you could
  use vegetable oil)

Soak the saffron in 1 tablespoon of the water for as long as possible. When you are ready to start the dough, mix the yeast and sugar with the remaining water. Put the flour and salt in a large bowl, make a well and add the yeast mixture and saffron threads with their soaking water. You'd be well advised to use an electric mixer fitted with a dough hook for this, as it makes mixing much easier and less messy.

Knead to a dough, place in a bowl and cover then allow to rise in a warm place until doubled in size. Knead in the lard. The dough will get sticky for a while (the same as brioche), but then suddenly it will form a wonderful glossy dough. When it does, knead in the currants then cover and put in a warm place until the dough is nearly doubled in volume.

Mix the caster sugar and cardamom in a large bowl and set to one side.

Heat the pork fat in a small saucepan or wok over high heat so you can deep fry. Ideally the oil will be about 170°C (325°F). If you don't have a thermometer, test with a little piece of bread: the bread should sizzle about 5 seconds after being dropped into the hot fat. Just be aware that you'll need to cook the doughnuts in a few batches to make sure they cook evenly and the fat doesn't cool down too much.

Tear off tablespoon-size pieces of the dough and carefully lower them into the fat. Use a slotted spoon to turn them over when they've browned well on one side and brown the other side. Drain on paper towel and dust them in the cardamom sugar while still hot. Serve immediately.

SADIE'S WALNUT & WHISKY BISCUITS

MAKES 30 SMALL BISCUITS

These small, unassuming biscuits, invented by my missus Sadie, are quite addictive. Only lightly sweet, the icing sugar coating gives a contrast to the nutty biscuit within.

120 g (4¼ oz) butter, softened
3 tablespoons caster (superfine) sugar
2 teaspoons whisky, or you could use 1 teaspoon natural vanilla essence
1 teaspoon salt
100 g (3½ oz) crushed walnuts
135 g (4¾ oz) plain (all-purpose) flour
icing (confectioners') sugar, for dusting

Preheat the oven to 150°C (300°F). Line a baking tray with baking paper and set aside.

Beat the butter and sugar together in a bowl with the whisky and salt until really, really pale. Fold in the walnuts and flour, taking care not to overmix and knock out the air.

Use a dessert spoon to scoop out even amounts and use your hands to gently roll the mixture into balls. Again, you're trying not to squash out all the air or have the biscuits melt in your hands. Place the balls about 5 cm (2 inches) apart on the prepared baking tray.

Bake in the centre of the oven for 20–25 minutes, turning halfway through, until they start to turn slightly golden. Cool, dust with icing sugar and serve with steaming tea or a good black coffee.

HAZELNUT & CHOCOLATE KISS BISCUITS

MAKES 10

Imagine roasted nuts in a shortbread-style biscuit, sandwiched
with bittersweet chocolate icing. Now stop imagining and get baking.

180 g (6¼ oz) butter, softened
50 g (1¾ oz) brown sugar, sifted
1 tablespoon very strong espresso
   coffee (or dissolved instant)
200 g (7 oz/1⅓ cups) plain
   (all-purpose) flour
50 g (1¾ oz) cornflour (cornstarch)
100 g (3½ oz) hazelnuts,
   roasted lightly and crushed
   but not too finely ground

Chocolate butter icing
50 g (1¾ oz) butter, softened
65 g (2½ oz) icing (confectioners')
   sugar, sifted
3 tablespoons unsweetened cocoa
   powder, sifted

Preheat the oven to 180°C (350°F). Line a baking tray with baking paper and set aside.

Beat the butter with the brown sugar and coffee until pale and fluffy. Add the
flour, cornflour and hazelnuts and stir with a wooden spoon until just combined. The
mixture can be quite soft, and if you're doing it in a warm room, you may need to
refrigerate it for a bit prior to rolling. Roll large teaspoonfuls of the mixture to make
about 20 evenly sized balls.

Place the balls on the prepared baking tray, 5 cm (2 inches) apart so that they
won't touch when cooked (they could swell a little as they bake). Use a fork or two
fingers to press them down so they flatten out to a little less than 1 cm (⅜ inch) in
height. Bake in the centre the oven for 12–15 minutes or until they start to brown
on the bottom and perhaps just start to colour on top. Turn the tray around halfway
through, if you think of it. Cool on the tray until firm, then on a wire rack.

To make the chocolate butter icing, beat the butter with the icing sugar and
cocoa until smooth. Spread onto half the cooled biscuits and sandwich with the
remaining halves while the icing is still soft.

If you and the family don't eat them all as soon as they're made, they are better
a few hours later when the icing has firmed somewhat. In that case, store the biscuits
in an airtight container.

HONEY BUNS

MAKES 24 DINNER ROLLS

While these buns are fragrant with honey, you can have them with savoury food, too; they're amazing with the bacon butties (page 20). Like brioche, they're easier to make if you have an electric mixer fitted with a dough hook. In its absence, simply work the mixture by hand, which is messier and will take a bit longer to get the texture right, but is rewarding in that lovely hands-on-dough kind of way. The slower you can rise the mixture, the better the end result.

550 g (1 lb 4 oz/3⅔ cups) plain (all-purpose) flour, plus extra for dusting
7 g (¼ oz/1 sachet) dried yeast
1 teaspoon salt
250 ml (9 fl oz/1 cup) lukewarm milk
125 ml (4 fl oz/½ cup) vegetable or light olive oil
1 egg

1 egg yolk, extra (reserve the eggwhite for the glaze, below)
2 tablespoons honey

Glaze

30 g (1 oz) caster (superfine) sugar
30 g (1 oz) butter
2 tablespoons honey
1 eggwhite

Pop the flour, yeast and salt in the bowl of an electric mixer fitted with a dough hook and mix to combine. Pour the warm milk, oil, egg, egg yolk and honey into a jug and whisk to combine.

With the mixer on low speed, slowly pour in the milk mixture and mix until a dough forms. Increase the mixer speed to the next click and knead until the dough is smooth, about 5 minutes. If kneading by hand, allow about 15 minutes.

Cover with a clean cloth and leave in a warm place for about an hour or until doubled in size. Longer is better, but don't overprove the bread or it will go a bit funny in texture.

Turn the dough onto a lightly floured surface. Punch down, cover and let rest for 10 minutes. Divide into 24 pieces and shape each one into a ball. Place 12 balls each onto two baking trays lined with baking paper or lightly floured.

Cover and let rise in a warm place until doubled in size, about 30 minutes. Preheat the oven to 180°C (350°F). Meanwhile, to make the glaze, combine the sugar, butter and honey in a small saucepan over low heat and stir until the sugar has dissolved. Allow to cool then whisk in the eggwhite. Brush onto the rolls.

Bake for 20–25 minutes until golden brown. For extra honey flavour, brush with additional warmed honey while they are still hot from the oven.

HAZELNUT & ALMOND BISCUITS

MAKES 35–40

I sometimes make this with 100 per cent almonds, but this variation works
well when I have wonderful hazelnuts that I get from a mate who lives just
up the road. These are quick to make: It'll take you 20 minutes, maybe
a little more.

125 g (4½ oz) butter, softened
135 g (4¾ oz) caster (superfine) sugar
1 egg
180 g (6¼ oz) plain (all-purpose) flour
1 teaspoon ground ginger
½ teaspoon ground nutmeg
½ teaspoon ground cloves
½ teaspoon baking powder
½ teaspoon salt
125 g (4½ oz) whole hazelnuts
35–40 whole almonds (about 50 g or 1¾ oz), for decorating

Preheat the oven to 180°C (350°F). Beat the butter and sugar together in a bowl until
pale and fluffy. Beat in the egg. In a separate bowl, mix the flour with the spices,
baking powder and salt, then fold into the butter mixture.

Pulse the hazelnuts in a food processor until you have a fine yet crumbly texture:
you don't want it consistently fine like a commercial hazelnut meal. Fold the hazelnuts
into the biscuit mixture.

Line two trays with baking paper and dot with about 1 tablespoon of mixture
at regular intervals, leaving 5 cm (2 inches) between for them to spread a little. Don't
be too neat about it. Press a whole almond into the top of each one so it flattens the
biscuit dough somewhat. Bake for 8–10 minutes until they start to tan up a little;
the hazelnuts will already have made the mix a dusky colour.

Remove from the oven and allow to set on the trays before transferring to a wire
rack to cool completely. Store in an airtight container.

SPICED BISCUITS
(ALMOST LIKE A PFEFFERNÜSSE)
MAKES 30

Friend Sue Plant made something similar to these for Christmas, and even though I think they're great in winter, they remind me of the European Christmas I've never had. So we serve them every December. I couldn't help myself and adapted Sue's recipe. This, I'm proud to say, is the result.

150 g (5½ oz) butter, softened
190 g (6¾ oz) dark brown sugar
1 egg
1 teaspoon natural vanilla essence
270 g (9½ oz) plain (all-purpose) flour
50 g (1¾ oz/½ cup) almond meal
½ teaspoon baking powder
1½ teaspoons ground black pepper
2 teaspoons ground cinnamon
½ teaspoon ground ginger
1 teaspoon ground nutmeg
¼ teaspoon ground cloves
¼ teaspoon salt
icing sugar mixture, for dusting

Preheat the oven to 180°C (350°F). Line two baking trays with baking paper and set aside. Beat the butter and sugar together until pale and fluffy, then beat in the egg and vanilla. Fold in the flour, almond meal, baking powder, spices and salt, then continue mixing just until the dough comes together.

Roll the dough into balls the diameter of a large coin (3 cm/1¼ inches) and place them about 5 cm (2 inches) apart on the prepared baking trays.

Bake for 12–15 minutes in the centre of the oven, turning the trays around about halfway through, until lightly browned.

Let them cool slightly on a wire rack and then roll in icing sugar mixture.

YOGHURT FLATBREAD

MAKES 4

I've been disappointed by so many bought flatbreads that I tried making my own. This one gets a lovely crisp, flaky texture from the yoghurt, and is pretty nice brushed with garlic-scented olive oil and nothing more. It's fab with the cevaps (page 104) and pretty much the perfect thing to have with hummus (page 64).

7 g (¼ oz/1 sachet) dried yeast
1 tablespoon tepid water (body temperature)
1 teaspoon sugar
200 g (7 oz) natural yoghurt
about 230 g (8¼ oz) plain (all-purpose) flour,
    plus extra for dusting
¼ teaspoon salt
vegetable oil, for greasing
melted butter or olive oil, for serving

Mix the yeast, water and sugar in a big bowl. Whisk in the yoghurt, then stir in the flour and salt. Knead on a well-floured board for 10 minutes, cover and allow to rise for 2 hours or so. Punch down, knead for 5 minutes and divide into 4 pieces. Very gently pull the dough to form 12 cm (4⅘ inch) rounds.

Cook under a super-hot griller (broiler)—I used a lightly oiled pan—or in a woodfired oven until brown on each side, turning over to cook evenly. Brush with a little butter or olive oil and serve, ideally while still warm.

You can also cook this on a chargrill on a barbecue, or even on a ridged pan. Lightly oil each side before cooking.

Summer means long grass. And plenty of cream.
Our days start and usually end with the
dairy girls, my favourite place to be.

GINGER CREAMS
MAKES 10 SANDWICHED BISCUITS

The pepper in the icing, strange as it sounds, brings out a more robust gingery flavour. These lovely, short biscuits have just enough spice to sparkle up your day.

180 g (6¼ oz) butter, softened
50 g (1¾ oz) brown sugar, sifted
½ teaspoon ground ginger
¼ teaspoon ground nutmeg
200 g (7 oz/1⅓ cups) plain (all-purpose) flour
50 g (1¾ oz) cornflour (cornstarch)

Ginger icing
50 g (1¾ oz) butter, softened
100 g (3½ oz) icing (confectioners') sugar, sifted
½ teaspoon ground ginger
pinch of ground white pepper
1 teaspoon lemon juice

Preheat the oven to 180°C (350°F). Line a baking tray with baking paper and set aside.

Beat the butter with the brown sugar, ginger and nutmeg until pale and fluffy. Sift in the dry ingredients and stir with a wooden spoon until just combined. Roll large teaspoonfuls of the mixture to make about 20 evenly sized balls.

Place on the prepared baking tray, 5 cm (2 inches) apart so that they won't touch when cooked (they could swell a little as they bake). Use two fingers to press them down so they flatten out to a little less than 1 cm (⅜ inch) in height. Uneven is good, it ensures they look homemade. Bake in the centre of the oven for 12–15 minutes, or until they start to brown on the bottom and perhaps just start to colour on top a fraction. Turn the tray around halfway through, if you think of it. Cool on the tray until firm, then on a wire rack.

To make the ginger icing, beat the butter with the icing sugar until smooth. Beat in the ginger, pepper and juice. Spread onto half the biscuits and sandwich with the remaining biscuits while the icing is still soft. Store in an airtight container.

HONEY & WALNUT BISCUITS

MAKES ABOUT 18 SMALL BISCUITS

These biscuits are a little like a honey Anzac, though the nuts do change things somewhat. You can make these without the nut on top, but it does add more of that lovely walnut flavour. For best results, shell your own nuts.

100 g (3½ oz) caster (superfine) sugar
70 g (2½ oz) honey
100 g (3½ oz) butter
150 g (5½ oz) lightly toasted walnuts, coarsely crushed
100 g (3½ oz/⅔ cup) self-raising flour
generous pinch of salt
100 g (3½ oz) rolled oats
roughly 100 g (3½ oz) walnut halves, for decorating

Preheat the oven to 170°C (325°F). Line a baking tray with baking paper and set aside.

Heat the sugar, honey and butter gently in a small saucepan just until the butter and honey are melted. Allow to cool well, though not so well that it all goes hard again.

Mix the crushed walnuts, flour, salt and oats in a big bowl, and stir in the honey butter mixture until just combined.

Take about 3 teaspoons of the mixture for each biscuit, roll between your hands and press onto the prepared baking tray. Do about nine biscuits per tray, leaving some room for them to spread a little. Press a walnut half or quarter into the top of each one. Bake for 12–17 minutes until a good golden colour, turning the trays around after about 8 minutes. Remove from the oven, allow to cool on the tray for 5 minutes, then transfer gently to wire racks to fully cool. Store in an airtight container.

THE ULTIMATE FLAKY SCONE

MAKES ABOUT 25 SCONES

Based loosely on a cross between an English scone and the American beaten biscuit, this is more flaky than most scones; so flaky, in fact, that sometimes they puff up so much they fall over while baking! The important bit is having the butter in bits, not finely rubbed in like normal pastry.

> 270 g (9½ oz) self-raising flour, plus extra for dusting
> ½ teaspoon salt
> 2 teaspoons sugar
> 80 g (2¾ oz) butter, chilled and cut into 5 mm (¼ inch) cubes
> 150 ml (5 fl oz) pure cream (35% fat)
> 50 g (1¾ oz) natural yoghurt
> milk, for brushing
> jam and lightly whipped cream, for serving

Preheat the oven to 220°C (425°F).

Put the flour, salt and sugar into a bowl and rub the butter just until it's about half rubbed in. You want some bigger bits of butter, too.

Add the cream and yoghurt and knead just until the dough comes together. Place on a floured board, and roll it hardly at all, then hit it with a rolling pin to make a 20 cm (8 inch) square, or similar. Fold the square in half, turn it around a quarter turn (so the left-hand side is now the front edge) and hit (and, if really necessary, roll) again until it is about 20 cm square. Fold once and turn again (in the same direction), hit or roll and repeat twice more. This hitting and folding manages to sandwich butter and air between the layers. Hit or roll one last time to create a nice evenly thick dough about 2 cm (¾ inch) high.

Cut out scones with a 4.5 cm (1¾ inch) scone cutter and lay them on a floured baking tray, close enough together so that the scones touch gently. Mash the remaining dough together after cutting to make another smaller piece, which you also cut into scones, and continue kneading and cutting until all the dough is used up. Brush the top of the scones with a little milk and bake for 10–15 minutes until starting to colour top and bottom. Cool well, pull apart and serve with jam and cream.

PORK FAT GRISSINI

MAKES 20 THIN GRISSINI

You can use any bread dough, even sourdough if you have it, but the addition of pork fat makes this heavenly. You could use some of the fat that comes to the top of the twice-cooked pork (page 99), too, by skimming it, letting it set in the fridge and scooping off the lard.

7 g (¼ oz/1 sachet) dried yeast
½ teaspoon sugar
170 ml (5½ fl oz/⅔ cup) tepid water (body temperature)
250 g (9 oz/1¾ cups) plain (all-purpose) flour (use strong flour
    if you can find it), plus extra for dusting
½–1 teaspoon salt, plus extra for serving
3 tablespoons pork fat

Dissolve the yeast and sugar in 1 tablespoon of the water. Put the flour and salt in a large bowl, make a well in the centre and add the yeast mixture and remaining water.

Knead to a dough, smother with the fat, cover and allow to rise in a warm place until it has doubled in size. Knead again to incorporate all the fat. (An electric mixer fitted with a dough hook makes this much easier and cleaner, I must say.)

Preheat the oven to 200°C (400°F). Line two baking trays with baking paper and set aside. Cut the dough into 20 evenly sized pieces and roll and stretch them out to make rustic-looking strands—about 30 cm (12 inches) long and thinner than a man's little finger—using plenty of flour so they don't stick as you do it.

I like to start baking them as I finish rolling each tray, as they tend to rise a bit while you roll. Bake in the oven for 10–15 minutes until golden brown and reasonably crisp. Sprinkle with salt to serve.

MODERN FRUIT MINCE TARTS

MAKES ABOUT 12

Yep, mince tarts. Not really summer food to those in the northern hemisphere, but because Christmas is in summer here, we do adore serving these a few times each December. I've been trying to recreate my Great-aunt Ann's mince tarts for years, and this is the closest I've come.

1 lemon, scrubbed	**Sweet shortcrust pastry**
1 apple, peeled and cored	160 g (5¾ oz) butter, softened
100 g (3½ oz) currants	125 g (4½ oz) icing
100 g (3½ oz) sultanas	(confectioners') sugar
(golden raisins)	1 teaspoon vanilla essence
100 g (3½ oz) brown sugar	250 g (9 oz) plain (all-purpose)
3 tablespoons brandy	flour
100 g (3½ oz) walnuts or almonds,	3 egg yolks
finely chopped	caster (superfine) sugar,
1–2 teaspoons mixed spice	for dusting (optional)

To make the fruit mince, juice the lemon, strain and reserve. Place the peel in cold water in a small saucepan, bring to the boil and simmer until soft enough to purée, about 45–60 minutes, changing the water twice. Drain well and purée.

Grate the apple coarsely and pop it in the strained lemon juice. Toss the currants, sultanas and sugar in brandy, warming gently in the oven to plump. Mix all of the ingredients together and allow to sit overnight if possible, in the fridge. Add more brandy if it looks dry (especially if you store it). You need half this quantity for one batch of tarts.

This pastry is very, very short and hard to work with, but the pay off is that it makes sensational little tarts. In a food processor, blend the softened butter with the icing sugar and vanilla essence just to combine; you're not trying to whip it. Pulse in the flour until crumbly, then pulse in 2 egg yolks. Tip the mixture out onto the workbench and knead just until it forms a dough. Refrigerate for at least 30 minutes; longer in warmer climes as it can be quite a sticky pastry.

Preheat the oven to 180°C (350°F). Roll the pastry in 2 batches between sheets of plastic wrap, until 3–5 mm (⅛–¼ inch) thick. Cut 12 rounds of pastry to line 12 rounded muffin tin holes. Gently press the pastry rounds in the holes. Top with a small spoonful of mince, then press the edges of the pastry towards the centre over the top of the mince and brush with the remaining egg yolk, or sprinkle with caster sugar. Bake towards the bottom of the oven (use the bottom element of the oven if possible) for about 15 minutes until the pastry is cooked and coloured slightly at the edges and base. Cool and serve, perhaps with whisky-scented whipped cream.

FAT RASCALS

MAKES 20

This Yorkshire classic is a cross between a biscuit and a currant scone.
I reckon they have to have some lard in them, or they simply aren't as good.
You could use all butter, if that's all you have on hand. (Note that using
margarine will really compromise the flavour).

450 g (1 lb) plain (all-purpose) flour
60 g (2¼ oz) brown sugar
½ teaspoon salt
100 g (3½ oz) lard, chilled
125 g (4½ oz) butter, chilled and diced
150 g (5½ oz) currants
160 ml (5¼ fl oz) milk, to moisten
about 2 tablespoons caster (superfine) sugar, for dusting

Preheat the oven to 200°C (400°F). Line two baking trays with baking paper and
set them aside.

Put the flour, sugar and salt in a bowl and rub in the lard and butter until it's
the texture of coarse breadcrumbs. Please don't be fussy about this; some bits that
are unevenly mixed will make the dough more flaky and interesting. Add the currants
and enough milk to form a nice textured dough.

Roll out to 1.5 cm (⅝ inch) thick. Cut into 7 cm (2¾ inch) rounds, place these on
the prepared baking trays, dust with caster sugar and bake in the centre of the oven
for about 10–15 minutes or until starting to turn golden on both top and bottom. Cool
well on the trays then on wire racks. Eat within two days for best results.

BROWN SUGAR & ALMOND BITES

MAKES 16 BISCUITS

While they may look a bit dark and gnarled, these are what the Italians may call *brutti ma buoni*—ugly but good—because they taste fantastic. I find the texture can vary a bit between crisp and chewy, but usually with a lovely crunchy outside.

150 g (5½ oz) roasted almonds
150 g (5½ oz/¾ cup lightly packed) dark brown sugar
generous pinch of salt
¼ teaspoon ground nutmeg (fresh if possible)
20 g (¾ oz) butter
1 eggwhite
1 tablespoon self-raising flour
icing (confectioners') sugar, for dusting

Preheat the oven to 160°C (315°F). Line two baking trays with baking paper and set them aside.

Pulse half the almonds in a food processor to a fine, meal-like texture. Pop them into a small saucepan. Pulse the remaining nuts in the food processor a few times to make coarsely crushed nuts. Add to the same saucepan as the meal, add the brown sugar, salt, nutmeg, butter and eggwhite and heat on low to just melt the butter.

Cool well, fold in the flour, then roll 2 teaspoons of mixture at a time into balls. Roll in the icing sugar to dust and place them 5 cm (2 inches) apart on the prepared baking trays (they'll probably spread a lot as they cook).

Bake for 15–20 minutes until starting to change colour. Cool well and store those you don't gobble up immediately in an airtight container.

CHAPTER

7

DRINKS

There are drinks, and then there are summer drinks, scented with elderflower. Or gin. Spiked with a little strawberry, or vodka. Heady with lemon, or rose geranium. Or given a bit of ice cream to make a proper, no-nasties spider.

An abundance of fruit lends itself to drink making. You can steep the flavour from excess strawberries to make a drink that will outlast the fruit itself: a liquid memory of the flavour to make you smile for a week or two after harvest (or longer, if you freeze the concentrate). When the raspberries are ripe; when the lemon tree is groaning; when the rhubarb needs to be trimmed; that's the time to make drinks. And if you end up with a little bit of prosecco in with your peaches, so be it.

We make our own cordials and syrups for summer drinks. In the evenings, we might spike our cordial or make something with a little bit of bite. We might even open a cool-climate chardonnay or pinot gris. But in the interests of hydration, we think it's important to keep the fridge stocked with liquid refreshments of all kinds.

MICHELLE'S WHITE PEACH & MINT SANGRIA

MAKES A WHOLE LOT: ENOUGH FOR 6–8 PEOPLE

When my friend Michelle suggested a white peach drink for the book, I thought about it for two seconds before having one of these and becoming a convert. It took quite a lot of tasting to be sure the recipe was just right, though. Which was the end of a very nice afternoon in the shade. You could make a smaller amount, but it really is a bit of a party drink, even if you are drinking alone.

3 white peaches
150 ml (5 fl oz) peach schnapps, or similar
2 mint sprigs
750 ml bottle of prosecco, chilled

Halve the peaches and remove the stones. Cut into thin wedges.

Place the peaches in a large jug or decanter with the schnapps and mint. Allow to macerate for 30 minutes at least, in the fridge. Ideally, leave it for a few hours in the fridge, even up to overnight.

When you're ready to drink, top up the jug with the prosecco, give the sangria a twizzle, and serve immediately in a medium glass, such as a tumbler.

REAL CHERRY JUICE SPIDER

PER PERSON

At some point the bright red spider (ice-cream soda) of my youth had to be reinvented. Ours uses proper cherry juice that we buy from a local cidery, some good-quality ice cream, and vanishes from sight in the first 2 minutes after making. The colour isn't as bright as the old version, which is probably a good thing.

50 ml (1¾ fl oz) unsweetened cherry juice
1 tablespoon caster (superfine) sugar
1 teaspoon lemon juice
100 ml (3½ fl oz) soda water (club soda)
1 scoop proper vanilla ice cream

Whisk the cherry juice with the sugar just to dissolve the sugar. Add the lemon juice and soda water, stir, then pour into a tall glass and plop in the ice cream. Serve immediately with one of those old-fashioned wax-coated paper straws for a real taste of nostalgia.

▼ ▼

If you can't find unsweetened cherry juice, you can use the syrup from other cordials in this book, such as raspberry and elderflower (page 239); strawberry and rose geranium (page 244); or even try rhubarb (page 243). Omit the sugar and lemon juice from this recipe if you do, because those syrups are already sweetened.

GROWN-UP STRAWBERRY SLUSHIE
MAKES 4

I've always been a fan of the iced fruit drink. So much so that it still reminds me of my childhood. But sometimes you want just a little more than fruit, sugar and water, and that's where this drink comes in. The amount of sugar I've given is a guide: let your taste determine how much to use because strawberries vary a lot in sweetness depending on season, location and variety. The vodka, however, is probably a bit more consistent.

250 g (9 oz) fresh strawberries, stems removed
2–3 tablespoons sugar
squeeze of lemon juice
50 ml (1¾ fl oz) Grand Marnier (orange-flavoured cognac liqueur)
25 ml (1 fl oz) vodka
2 small basil leaves, washed
350 g (12 oz) ice, crushed

Liquidise or purée the strawberries with the sugar in a blender or food processor. Add the remaining ingredients and pulse until slushy. Serve immediately in four daiquiri or martini glasses.

KAFFIR LIME & LEMON CORDIAL

MAKES ROUGHLY 1.5 LITRES (52 FL OZ/6 CUPS), ENOUGH FOR ABOUT 4–5 LITRES (140–175 FL OZ/16–20 CUPS) OF DRINK

I adore the aroma of kaffir limes, but they're notoriously hard to juice. So, here, we harness the fragrance, add a bit of lemon for acid, and liven it up with a little ginger, too. Some might find the zest a little odd, but I think it adds a lovely 'real' character to the cordial.

4 lemons, scrubbed

4 medium kaffir lime leaves

3 mm (⅛ inch) slice of fresh ginger,
   bruised with the back of a knife

700 g (1 lb 9 oz) caster (superfine) sugar

1 litre (35 fl oz/4 cups) boiling water

50 g (1¾ oz) tartaric acid (if you can't get tartaric acid, use about
   a quarter of the quantity of citric acid [sour salt])

Finely grate the zest of the lemons and juice the flesh, reserving the squeezed halves. Put the lemon juice, grated zest and reserved lemon halves with the lime leaves and the ginger slice into a very large bowl or heatproof container and add the caster sugar. Tip in the boiling water and stir until dissolved. Leave to cool overnight, popping in the fridge if it's a very warm night.

Remove the lemon halves, lime leaves and ginger, stir in the tartaric acid and pour into sterile bottles. Refrigerate until ready for use and shake before pouring. You'll need about 2–3 tablespoons of this syrup to flavour each tall glass of water.

RASPBERRY & ELDERFLOWER CORDIAL

MAKES 1 LITRE (35 FL OZ/4 CUPS) CORDIAL, ENOUGH FOR ABOUT 3–4 LITRES (105–140 FL OZ/12–16 CUPS) OF DRINK

This one is bright and fresh and gorgeously pink. A similar drink can be made using strawberries if you have them.

> 300 g (10½ oz) fresh or frozen raspberries
> 2 tablespoons elderflower cordial (concentrate)
> 500 g (1 lb 2 oz) caster (superfine) sugar
> 1 small fresh bay leaf
> 1 litre (35 fl oz/4 cups) boiling water
> 1 tablespoon citric acid (sour salt)

Pop the raspberries, elderflower, sugar and bay leaf in a large bowl. Add the boiling water and stir well to make sure the sugar has all dissolved. Leave this to sit overnight, then strain through a fine sieve, allowing gravity to do the work. Don't force the pulp through the sieve (you can use it for pancakes and other things, though). Whisk the citric acid into the raspberry syrup, and store in sterile bottles in the fridge.

There's the rustle of grass, the crunch underfoot.
We get up early to do chores so we don't bake,
though even then, we work up a thirst.

RHUBARB CORDIAL

MAKES 1 LITRE (35 FL OZ/4 CUPS) AND A BIT

We have a surplus of rhubarb in summer, so we've started making cordial. This concentrated syrup goes really well with soda and ice, but a touch of vodka makes the grown-ups happy. And sleepy.

  1 bunch rhubarb stems, about 800 g (1 lb 12 oz), washed well
  600 g (1 lb 5 oz) caster (superfine) sugar
  2 lemons, scrubbed and halved
  1 litre (35 fl oz/4 cups) boiling water
  2 tablespoons citric acid

Give the rhubarb a quick hit with the back of a knife along each stem. Cut it into 3 cm (1¼ inch) lengths and put in a bowl big enough to hold it all plus the boiling water. Add the sugar and gently squeeze the lemons in, adding the squeezed lemon halves too.

Pour over the boiling water, stir well to dissolve the sugar, then leave it to stand for 24 hours, covering if need be to keep out dust and bugs.

Strain the cordial into another bowl or big jug and whisk in the citric acid. (I keep the spent rhubarb to use in desserts, but remember it's only a shadow of its former self; the whole point has been to extract a lot of the rhubarb flavour.)

Pour the cordial into sterile bottles and store in the fridge until ready to use, for up to about a month. You'll know it's gone off when it starts to pop as you open the bottle because it's beginning to ferment...though for a few days you could pretend it's your very own rhubarb wine.

Use the cordial to taste, but work on about one part cordial to three parts soda or tonic water.

STRAWBERRY & ROSE GERANIUM CORDIAL

MAKES ABOUT 1 LITRE (35 FL OZ/4 CUPS) CORDIAL, ENOUGH FOR 3–4 LITRES (105–140 FL OZ/12–16 CUPS) OF DRINK

You can use frozen fruit for this, as it breaks down better in the hot water and releases just as much, if not more, flavour.

> 500 g (1 lb 2 oz) very ripe strawberries
> 2 lemons, scrubbed
> 2 rose geranium leaves
> 500 g (1 lb 2 oz) caster (superfine) sugar
> 1 litre (35 fl oz/4 cups) boiling water

Put the strawberries in a large bowl. Squeeze the lemons and add both the juice and the squeezed halves to the bowl with the rose geranium leaves and sugar. Pour over the boiling water and stir well to dissolve the sugar. Leave overnight, for at least 12 hours, then strain out the fruit. Don't press the fruit through a sieve, just let it drain under gravity, which can take a while but gives the best result. Refrigerate the cordial and water down to about one-third or one-quarter of the original strength.

WATERMELON BASIL GIN FIZZ

MAKES ABOUT 6 DRINKS

Nothing says summer like a big chunk of watermelon; and nothing says summer like a big glass of watermelon and basil drink, laden with ice and laced with gin. Here's Fat Pig's favourite way to use watermelon in a glass.

¼ seedless watermelon, cut into chunks
1 tablespoon white wine vinegar
60 ml (2 fl oz/¼ cup) Basil Sugar Syrup (see below)
600 ml (21 fl oz) soda water (club soda)
gin, to taste
basil leaves, for serving

Basil sugar syrup
250 ml (9 fl oz/1 cup) water
100 g (3½ oz/½ cup) sugar
handful of basil leaves

To make the basil sugar syrup, combine the water and sugar in a small saucepan over medium heat and stir until the sugar dissolves. Bring to the boil then remove from the heat and add the basil leaves. Set aside and allow to cool while the basil infuses into the syrup. (After you've made your drinks, refrigerate the extra basil sugar syrup in clean jars for up to 2 weeks or until the next round.)

To make the cordial, pop the watermelon, vinegar and the basil sugar syrup into a blender and purée until smooth. Pour the mixture through a fine sieve set over a bowl or jug to strain out any pips and foam.

To make the gin fizz, fill a glass with ice, pour in some watermelon cordial to about a third of the way up, add a splash of gin then top with soda water. Garnish with basil leaves.

ELDERFLOWER & GIN SPARKLERS
(PINK GRAPEFRUIT JUICE WITH
ELDERFLOWER, SODA & GIN)
PER PERSON

Yep, that's a good thing. Something you can knock up in a jiffy that lightens the mood, brightens the personality (at least that's what Sadie tells me) and finishes the day on a good note.

juice of 1 pink grapefruit
juice of ¼ lemon (about 1 teaspoon)
1–2 teaspoons elderflower cordial (concentrate)
30 ml (1 fl oz) gin (for grown-ups, that is)
100 ml (3½ fl oz) soda water (club soda)

Mix all of the ingredients together and serve over a little crushed ice in a glass. Often.

WHITE PEACH, GIN & BASIL DRINK

PER PERSON

So, it's hot, is it? And you need a little something that tastes of the season? Luckily, you can turn one peach into about eight drinks and toast the long summer days.

> 125 ml (4 fl oz/½ cup) soda water (club soda)
> 1 basil leaf
> 30 ml (1 fl oz) Peach Purée (see below)
> 30 ml (1 fl oz) gin

> **Peach purée**
> (makes enough for about 8 drinks)
> 1 large white peach, skin and stone removed
> 2 tablespoons sugar
> 50 ml (1¾ fl oz) water
> a little squeeze of lemon juice

To make the peach purée, cut the peach flesh into wedges and heat them in a small saucepan with the sugar and water until just soft, adding the lemon juice to taste. Press through a very fine sieve, discarding any solids. Chill before using, ideally.

To make the drink, simply mix all of the ingredients, perhaps adding a touch of lemon juice and ice to taste, in a tall glass. Then toast the season.

INDEX

Page numbers in **bold** refer to photographs.

ACKNOWLEDGMENTS

This book is my love letter to summer. To the season that has us casting off layers of clothes and rejoicing in longer days. The hot season that always delights with bounty from the ground, even when it sometimes threatens to break our hearts and test our resolve. For inspiration I have to thank nature. That strange, recalcitrant, impossibly complex being that determines what will happen on our farm at the bottom end of Australia. Weather. The change in seasons that happens from one month to the next, meaning every crop, every variety of fruit, every thing we use in our kitchen and put in our mouth is a reflection of the remarkable place in which we live.

The recipes in *Summer on Fat Pig Farm* are the result of what nature brings us. But the book is more than just that. It's made exquisitely beautiful by the photography of Alan Benson, a gifted, humorous mate for all seasons. It's brought to life thanks to the styling of good buddy, talented cook and all round Fat Pig helper, Michelle Crawford. (Gratitude, also, to Michelle's family for letting us take over her kitchen while our new farmhouse was being built.) And the food looks good enough to pluck off the page, thanks to being cooked delectably by the seemingly always-chipper Kellie McChesney. (I also greatly appreciated the Series 2 Land Rover, so cheers to Geoffrey Lewis for the loan.)

I'm incredibly indebted to Sue Hines from Murdoch Books for having faith in me, yet again, to produce a book of substance. To the ever-patient, ever-persuasive and always lovely publisher Jane Morrow; yes, I do love the sound of deadlines as they rush by. For getting the words to make more sense than I could do alone, and for bringing out the best in the recipes, it's a big thumbs up to Barbara McClenahan and Melody Lord, and for the lovely country-feeling design, thank you to Dan Peterson and Jacqui Porter.

A farm is all about community. I'd like to express my heartfelt appreciation to the good folk of our beloved Huon Valley for showing me the way. For helping pull in the hay when it's about to rain (I'm talking about you and the boys, Michael), for helping butcher the sheep (Gerard), the pigs (Marty, David, Todd and James at various times), for making truly great ham and bacon (Ben), and for watching out for us as we make our way in the world. We're indebted to the Canes for their melting flesh peaches. To Mary for the cherries. To Marshall for the black currants. To Dave for the strawberries. And to all the other growers for the inspiration, the motivation and the occasional invitation to see what they grow and how they produce food from the soil.

Our family run holding, Fat Pig Farm, is only possible because of the love, commitment and passion of one person—my wife, Sadie. The farm is our biggest joy, the greatest pride, the most work and the scariest project we've encountered. As we put down deep roots in our little gully, as we nurture the soil, the seedlings, the biodiversity, it is only with a hand to hold, a shoulder to lean on and a back for support that I am able to do what I do. We have crazy dreams. We still want more for our farm, for our valley, for our son and the other sons and daughters of the Huon. But at Fat Pig Farm, we already live the dream. It's our hope that others will follow their desires to get closer to the soil, too.

Published in 2015 by Murdoch Books, an imprint of Allen & Unwin

Murdoch Books Australia
83 Alexander Street
Crows Nest NSW 2065
Phone: +61 (0) 2 8425 0100
Fax: +61 (0) 2 9906 2218
murdochbooks.com.au
info@murdochbooks.com.au

Murdoch Books UK
Erico House, 6th Floor
93–99 Upper Richmond Road
Putney, London SW15 2TG
Phone: +44 (0) 20 8785 5995
murdochbooks.co.uk
info@murdochbooks.co.uk

For Corporate Orders & Custom Publishing contact
Noel Hammond, National Business Development Manager, Murdoch Books Australia

Publisher: Jane Morrow
Editorial Manager: Barbara McClenahan
Design Manager: Hugh Ford
Project Editor: Melody Lord
Designers: Dan Peterson and Jacqui Porter, Northwood Green
Photographer: Alan Benson
Stylist: Michelle Crawford
Home Economist: Kellie McChesney
Production Manager: Mary Bjelobrk

A cataloguing-in-publication entry is available from the catalogue of the National Library of Australia
at nla.gov.au.

ISBN 978 1 74336 579 3 Australia
ISBN 978 1 74336 580 9 UK

A catalogue record for this book is available from the British Library.

Colour reproduction by Splitting Image Colour Studio Pty Ltd, Clayton, Victoria
Printed by 1010 Printing International Limited, China

IMPORTANT: Those who might be at risk from the effects of salmonella poisoning (the elderly, pregnant women, young children and those suffering from immune deficiency diseases) should consult their doctor with any concerns about eating raw eggs.

OVEN GUIDE: You may find cooking times vary depending on the oven you are using. For fan-forced ovens, as a general rule, set the oven temperature to 20°C (35°F) lower than indicated in the recipe.

MEASURES GUIDE: We have used 20 ml (4 teaspoon) tablespoon measures. If you are using a 15 ml (3 teaspoon) tablespoon add an extra teaspoon of the ingredient for each tablespoon specified.